Praise

"Soorya Townley's honest account as she walks us through the midst of her horrific tragedy, is somehow also filled with spirit, humor and wisdom."

Patrice Karst, bestselling author of The Invisible String series

"How do we measure bottomless grief? What makes this true story so gripping resides less in the outer combats—that are astounding in themselves—but Soorya's honest and eloquent rendering of her all-too-human inner processes of sorrow, rage, compassion, skillfulness and love contribute so mightily to the final outcome."

Marvin Treiger, PhD, Marriage & Family Therapist (Ret.), teacher of Buddhism and Tai Qi

About the Author

Soorya Townley, born near Detroit, Michigan, moved to Los Angeles at age eight and survived years of domestic violence. As an adult, she raised two children and had three husbands. She pursued careers as a hairdresser, Astrologer, and Numerologist, singing telegrams, and composed music and poetry. Her longest career has been in massage therapy while simultaneously becoming a writer and a professional editor.

SOORYA TOWNLEY

RIPPLES *in the* RIVER

Ripples in the River

Print Edition
ISBN: 978-3-98832-159-6
Published by Vine Leaves Press 2025

Cover design by Jessica Bell
Interior design by Amie McCracken

To Erika and Charla

Despite the evil that falls our way,
we must be like soldiers and keep holding the light.

Author's Note

Everything in my book is as close to memory as possible. All names, except for a few of the police, are the real names. It all began when my granddaughter said, "I've heard the other family's side of the story, but you haven't shared yours." One day, walking along the beach in Africa as I wept for my loss, I thought, why not? Why not write everything that occurred so that my story can be told?

Chapter 1
Day of the Deed

Monday, June 12, 2006

As I drove the freeway in Ventura, California, singing along to Linda Ronstadt's "You're No Good" on the radio, my daughter Charla was being stabbed by her husband five hundred miles north in Reno, Nevada. Little did I realize how eerily close the song's lyrics were to my daughter's broken relationship with her husband: "I learned my lesson. It left a scar. Now I see who you really are ..."

Premonitions often come to me, but not on this day. My thoughts were focused on visiting my stepmother, who I had not seen in a long time. I rolled the car window down, and a crisp air blew against my face. The emerging sun spread across the dawn morning sky, piercing the puffy clouds.

My phone rang, and in an instant, my whole world was turned upside down. It was my daughter's neighbor, Kelli.

"Soorya! Did you hear the news? They're saying Darren shot Judge Weller! Oh my God, Soorya, do you know if Charla is okay?"

Waves of anxiety hit my heart while my fingers gripped the steering wheel. "No. Your call is the first I've heard of this. Would you try reaching her again and tell her to hide?"

"I already called her. She didn't answer." Kelli's voice pitched higher. I heard her panting as if jogging.

"Kelli, I'm hanging up now; I'll contact the police."

I reached for my water bottle on the passenger's seat, but I was too weak to twist the top. Darren, my troubled son-in-law, was now suspected of shooting the family court judge assigned to his and my daughter's divorce case, and it had already hit the press. I knew instantly he was responsible. Sometimes intuition is such that one doesn't need concrete proof. A solid sense of understanding from within reveals the truth.

Someone laid on their horn as I abruptly swerved through two lanes of traffic to get to the right lane.

After multiple unanswered calls, the Reno Police Department finally picked up. "You are in the wrong department." I was put on hold until someone else picked up. "I'm sorry. What is your daughter's name again? Could you spell it slowly, and who do you wish to speak to?" Being left adrift was agonizing. I finally reached a sympathetic officer. "Ma'am, I understand your problem. I'll get a squad car over to your daughter's house right away. What's her address?"

"I don't know." My thoughts scattered. "She just moved. Can you give me a minute to find it?"

"Take your time."

Take my time? I have no time to take. I reached for my purse and found her new address on a piece of paper inside one pocket. "Here ... it's here."

My hurried words stumbled so much that the officer slowed me down and made me repeat the address. Once finished, I continued calling Charla. When I heard her voice recording message I wanted to reach out and pull her to safety. But all I got was a recording. Why hadn't I stayed with her this week after the conclusion of a long, bitterly fought divorce? Now, I was powerless.

I desperately needed to call every friend in Reno to check on my girl, but I couldn't manage to pull over, so I headed home. It wasn't like Charla to not pick up the phone. I crossed two fingers until they hurt, hoping my daughter used her instincts to hide. *Please be safe, my precious baby. If Darren was demonic enough to shoot a judge, he's crazy enough to come for you …*

Twenty minutes had passed since Kelli's call. I scrolled through my contacts and found Lisa's number, Charla's best friend and maid of honor. If anyone knew where she was, it would be her. My stomach cramped in a moaning pain.

"Lisa, it's Soorya. I just heard from Charla's neighbor. She is concerned Charla is in danger. Have you heard from her?"

"Where are you?" Lisa answered a question with a question, and her voice was flat, which worried me.

"Driving the freeway."

"I'll call in a while …"

Lisa sounded fainter, further away. I'd never heard her like that and thought it odd she asked where I was.

After five minutes, I couldn't stand it and pushed her number again. No response. On the third attempt, she picked up. "Lisa, I can't wait—can you tell me anything? I need to know."

"He fucking killed her." Lisa's voice erupted into a fierce growl. "He killed her before he shot the judge."

Chapter 2
The First Night

It's impossible to remember how my conversation with Lisa ended, or how I safely made it home. My fixated, zombie-like eyes stared blankly ahead through the clear windshield as my cracked heart sunk into an endless pool of pouring rain. I yearned to slide barefoot through wet layers of leaves inside a thick forest. If I reached down and touched the ground's texture while looking up at the sky, would I have sensed the intelligence of creation feeling sympathy for me? Something told me all I could be was one particle. My life didn't matter. Nothing mattered except my granddaughter.

I impulsively called Bruce, a psychologist who worked with me at a drug and alcohol rehabilitation center in Malibu. I didn't know why I called him, because we had bickered two weeks before. I overheard him tell a patient that women attack men more often than men hurt women. His comment annoyed me, as most women's assaults go unreported. As soon as I heard his voice, my impulse was to click off. Instead, "Bruce, can you help me?"

"Soorya, what's wrong?"

"My daughter's been murdered, and I'm driving. Can't feel my body."

"Okay, take a deep breath and feel your toes. Take another breath."

The deeper breathing helped. "Thanks. I'll take it from here."

I could not think of anyone else to contact. There was no one in the world to save me. I was on my own.

I was able to arrive at my condominium and park, but I couldn't make myself open the car door. My head rested on the steering wheel while I waited to weep. The crisp morning air was gone and it was now 100 degrees. Loud wood-chipper sounds grated through the neighborhood. A man worked on a utility pole in front of me. Dogs barked back and forth. Life looked like yesterday. If only it were …

Sweat poured down my face. My underarms soaked with perspiration. I stared at the air conditioning button—was it even a foot away from me? I had no strength to turn it on. Usually, the first effort I make is to control the temperature. Now I controlled nothing.

After twenty minutes, I forced my hand to open the car door as I felt myself moving forward on the pavement to my apartment. Once inside, I called Lisa again. "How did you find out?"

"I reached Charla's lawyer, Shawn Meador's office. Secretaries always spill the beans. She said that the police determined Darren did it. But they need DNA proof …"

"Wouldn't they call him a person of interest?"

"Yeah, but I'm not sure what the procedure is for the police informing the families. Has anyone contacted you?"

"Nothing. When I called, no one even knew who my daughter was. The police must have found evidence since it's now blaring on the radio."

"Okay." Lisa sighed. "Once I heard about Charla, I stopped contacting anyone. I caved."

A vein in my neck pulsed. I wished Lisa and I could have been in the same room. Instead, we were two desolate islands, miles apart, unraveling the facts about our Charla.

"Just a minute," Lisa said, and it sounded like she held the phone to the side. "Jamie! I'm on the phone! Excuse me, Soorya."

So much for Lisa being a desolate island—somehow, I'd forgotten she had children. Jamie, her eight-year-old daughter, was the same age as Erika, Charla's daughter and at that time my only grandchild. Another impact hit me like a sudden whack: Erika's step-brother and step-sister would find out. As would her friends and classmates. How could the news not stun and devastate them?

Lisa broke my trance. "Oh, I forgot. The police went to Shawn's office. You know who Shawn is—right?"

"Charla's lawyer."

"The police warned him to drop everything and to come in and pick up a bulletproof vest. Now he's in hiding."

We hung up. Nothing more to say - our beloved Charla was dead. Our conversation was one of the most frustrating I'd ever had. Invisible weights were working to suffocate our spirits.

As I lay on the couch until dark, I continued aching for Lisa's plight along with my own. Even though my loss was horrible, I had a burning compassion for hers. She and Charla had been inseparable. They'd taken seminars together, aligned pregnancies, and gone on vacations away from their husbands. I'd never experienced two women having more fun than Lisa and Charla. This was catastrophic for her. And because of her youth, she was even more affected than me. Blood isn't always thicker than water. When water comes up from the earth, it is a source of vitality and, aside from our breath, it is the life source that connects us. These two women had nurtured each other like soul sisters.

I went into the bathroom and slid to the floor. The cold linoleum offered some relief from the searing day's heat. I touched the toilet. It felt solid enough to stabilize me. My hand reached over, lifted the handle, and flushed. As I watched the water rush down the drain, it helped to wash away my thoughts as well. I looked at my lower leg. Under the skin, there was an area covered with bubbles. I wondered if this was shingles. I marveled at how fast the body reacts to trauma.

Hobbling to the living room, I remembered to call Marilyn, my friend of three decades. As I told her the news, my hand shook so badly I dropped the phone twice. My cheap K-mart beige clock on the wall helped me focus. Within minutes, Marilyn was at my house. "Soorya, do you need me to go to Reno with you?"

Lost in floaty feelings somewhere within, I heard myself say, "No, that's okay. I don't want to inconvenience you. I'll be fine."

"You are out of touch, my darling. I'm going with you." Marilyn took my hand and gently squeezed it. "And I'm not leaving your side. All you have to do is get to my house tomorrow morning, and I'll take over from there. I already called my brother, Michael, and he's helping us with frequent flyer miles."

I hated the thought of someone giving up their travel credits, but I surrendered. The idea of booking a flight was impossible. Press two, press four, etc., then following instructions and pulling a credit card out—no. I tried to express how sweet that was of her brother, but I couldn't do it. It would be a fifteen-minute drive to Marilyn's house, and I foresaw parallel parking on her street. When I first learned to drive as a teen, I visualized how I would travel into areas the day before to make sure I landed correctly. Now, I was uncertain of movements beyond my body. But I had to take the risk since I needed my car once I arrived back. My friend had done enough. As Marilyn opened the door to leave, it was dusk outside.

Within seconds of being alone I found a large framed photo of a smiling Charla and placed it on the coffee table. In the kitchen, I removed a huge purple candle from a box still unpacked from just moving in the week before and lit the wick with a match. Charla's head was tilted to one side and her bright eyes gleamed with tenderness. The fire represented her essence and held energy for all who grieved. I'd been to ashrams for meditation, burned candles at the altars of Catholic churches in Rome, sat by roaring fires after sweat lodges with American Indians in Arizona, and prayed during elaborate Hindu puja ceremonies. This candle had more meaning than any I had ever held or lit. No ceremony or gathering came close to the significance and depth of pure devotion that this luminosity held for me that night for my daughter. Its flame became my center. Outdoor lamps turned on and shone through my living room window. Those lights made me remember reading about priests exorcising demons. I thought of Darren.

Next, there was the dreaded call to my son Christopher, who was overseas on a temporary assignment with the U.S. Embassy in New Delhi, India. He'd been there for only three months, and my daughter-in-law, Genicia, arrived the week before. Christopher had just given Genicia a long-awaited diamond ring in the inner sanctum of the Taj Mahal.

"Hi, Mom. How are you?"

"Christopher, I have some horrible news, sweetheart. Are you sitting down? If not, please do." My flat tone now resembled Lisa's.

"Mom, this sounds serious."

Christopher and I always made playful jokes when talking. I would blurt something funny or quirky and Christopher would say, "Hold on until I get my book!" He'd write what I said, and giggle as he scrawled. I told friends we had the gift to hit each other's funny bone. There was no humor now. Nothing to write down so we could laugh. Every somber word would be seared into our souls.

Christopher adored his sister, and I was afraid he might have a nervous breakdown because of what Charla had endured.

"Darren killed my baby! He killed your sister. She's gone."

"What … Mom … for real?"

My breathy voice whispered, "Yes. I'm so, so sorry to relate this to you long distance."

I kept apologizing, but the words were like flimsy decorating paper spilling wildly from a breezy, open window. Everything in the material world scattered. Christopher held the phone away from his mouth. "Geni, Darren murdered my sister!"

Genicia screamed so loud I imagined a laser beam hitting its target. Christopher sobbed into the phone.

"I'm not sure what's next, but I have to hurry and get custody of Erika, then figure things out."

"Of course, Mom. I'm going to quit my position here and come to stay with you. Geni and I will pack up and fly to Reno as fast as we can."

"But you just started your post ..."

"You need help, Mom, and I want to be there for you both. I can always get something else."

"What about your belongings?"

"We'll leave most of our things here and have someone mail them to us."

I couldn't grasp the complications of moving back and forth from across the world. My mind still wrestled with driving to Marilyn's.

After our goodbyes, I forced myself to pack clothing. I added a toothbrush, floss, and shampoo into a soft-sided toiletry case, and stuffed it into the corner of the bag. The possibility of needing formal outfits to look professional for lawyers, court, or anything else didn't occur. No thinking of packing makeup or taking another pair of shoes. I did place in a black sweater and a black dress for the funeral. The funeral: Oh, Father-Mother God. My stiff body went back to sitting on the couch watching the lit candle on the coffee table, then staring at Charla's photo.

Just as the phone rang, the clock ticked 10:30 pm. I answered. "Hello?"

"Is this Soorya Townley?"

"Yes."

"My name is Kim Garrett. I work for the Reno Police Department for victims of crime. What I have to say is hard for me; I have to inform you we have positively identified your daughter as the murder victim."

"Yes, I know. Charla's friend contacted me and said it was her."

Still devoid of tears, I was steel at my core.

"First, I want to say how sorry I am for your loss." Kim continued. "I've been assigned to help to get you situated and to assist you in any way I can. I will take care of your living arrangements and will drive you around for your necessary travel. Are you flying?"

"Yes, I'll be there tomorrow morning, Southwest, with a friend. Where's Erika?"

Kim's voice shifted softer. "She's with Darren's mother, Joan Mack, staying at her house. I'm glad to hear you are coming in right away. I'll text you so you have my contacts."

"Sure. Has anyone told Erika?"

"Yes, Charla's father, your ex, Jan, was here too. A detective said that Jan and Joan took Erika aside a half hour ago into a room and informed her."

I suspected Kim was nervous as her voice hesitated, and she had stumbled on Jan's first name.

Jan, with his second wife, Jackie, lived in Reno. As soon as Charla and Darren married, Charla asked Darren to give her father a position at Palace Jewelry and Loan, Darren's family business. Jan had worked there for ten years, helping them make internet sales. Even though Jan was my former husband, we had been a comfortable, extended family and even hung out together at Charla's pool parties. My mind lingered on what it must have been like for Jan, sitting at his desk inside the Mack family store, hearing the news announced from the radio that Darren was a suspect in the shooting of Judge Weller. But that wouldn't be the worst news Jan would hear. Soon, the police would inform him about his daughter.

Kim spoke. "I've rented you a motel room in another name, so you will have anonymity."

"Thank you." My tone remained lifeless.

"The press will look for a statement from you."

"Oh, that's right—reporters."

"I need to go now, but I'll be waiting for you as soon as you get off the plane." Kim gave me her cell number and then we said our goodbyes.

I wondered if Kim was younger than my daughter, and if it was her fate to give me the tragic news. Chills grabbed me despite the blistering weather.

My apartment was now foreign; every object I owned felt unnecessary and invasive. I wished I owned nothing but a table, a bowl, and a pillow. Thinking about food repulsed me. The night before, I'd watched the finale of American Idol, and wept for joy. It was the most beautiful season. I quickly called Charla afterward and said, "You *have* to see it."

Charla cheered. "Oh boy, I'll eat two bowls of ice cream at the same time!"

I promised to mail her a taped recording of the show. We always shared our significant experiences. Sometimes we'd talk three or four times a day.

Now, television appeared superficial, disgusting. I glanced at the blank, meaningless screen. I doubted I'd ever watch it again. My only interest, aside from the candle and Charla's photo, was to sit on the couch and cling to tiny flaws in the room. I saw specks on the walls, on furniture, everywhere. It was surprising how many thousands of bits there were. Every material substance contained them. Looking around, I had never realized how deeply imperfect the world was. Any smudge held my attention and subdued me. Those spots were a trusted companion to rest on, without sacrifice. They took nothing from me and gave nothing back, which became a safe place to land. I circled them, over and over and over, like they were the most important thing to do, the only thing to do if I wanted to hold on to my sanity.

Chapter 3
Dreams and Visions

Immeasurable feelings poured through my exhausted emptiness as I lay near-comatose in the dark. My blown-apart world ached to be glued back together. I ached for my son and an *alive daughter* to be laughing in the next room. I wanted to smell our favorite popcorn made with truffle oil, nutritional yeast and lemon as we sat and munched, taking turns grabbing into the same wooden bowl from the coffee table. But only ashes remained, with death oozing its filthy fluid and drowning everything. A chant kept ringing in my head:

Darren Mack, husband-father-friend, has chosen the path of wickedness inside of sin.

A failed human had blindsided us with his most wicked act. But he would never reach inside the one pocket of my heart which contained a stone made of light. That eternal shining substance would sustain me, and it was more powerful than any violence he could commit.

Throughout that evening, all I managed to do was to press one hand on my heart while imagining that stone, then kneeling at the coffee table to adore my daughter's photo.

Charla's smile seemed surreal now. I picked up her picture and traced a finger across her beautiful face. It had always been thrilling to enjoy her sincere smile and soul-revealing eyes. As soon as she was around, she'd think of a clever comment to entertain anyone she was with. One of her friends I'd bumped into previously at a deli counter in LA marveled, "Charla came over last week and fixed our television. She got out the directions to the remote, sat patiently for what seemed like hours, and then wrote simple directions on colored notebook paper she'd brought. She even drew icons of funny faces for each step."

I remembered how once Darren moved out of their house last winter, he turned off the utilities, registered in his name, for spite. Charla couldn't get them back on without his permission. There was a fireplace in the den and she pretended for Erika's sake like they were camping, by bringing out two sleeping bags and attempted to make the situation fun. By the third night Charla had to rent a hotel because they were too cold since the room had faulty insulation. Charla finally called Darren's mother and she made him turn the utilities back on.

As I sat on the couch reviewing those memories, much like a famished person grasping for that last drink of water, the clock's hand settled at midnight. I desperately wanted to communicate with Charla's spirit–somewhere, somehow. Yet, my mind couldn't stop imagining my daughter's lifeless body lying limp on an ice-cold slab inside a morgue.

My apartment was filled with a hazy, gray fog everywhere I looked. It transferred and spread like malice, permeating even the furniture. Something in me accepted that sight as normal, evil had already won that day.

I was witnessing shock and marveled at its mistiness emanating through my eyes.

This has to be my brain helping me adjust to trauma.

A steady part of me studied it. Even though I had accepted evil had taken my daughter, I mentally gripped the sacred stone in my heart for more to come.

At three a.m., I moved my body back to bed, fell asleep, and entered a lucid dreaming state. I saw and heard myself standing somewhere in the universe saying, "I'd like to speak with my daughter, Charla."

My voice had an unusually lower, sludge-like register, firmly commanding results. A greenish-blue form appeared in front of me. It was Charla. We intermeshed in a quick embrace, but my earthly self could not detect what we said. Our encounter seemed long in the other dimension, but short in ours. The most significant understanding was that I knew she was still alive. I couldn't see any detailed form, just a vivid green-blue color. The Indian guru named Amma once taught that green is a healing frequency, and if the crossed-over being permeates it, they are beginning the process of reintegrating their trauma and wounds.

There was love, yet it seemed more like we were sorting things out. In my dream state, I knew all was as it should be, even though that knowledge was without a drop of joy.

When I woke up my legs were tangled in the sheets. Even though elated I had just united with my former daughter, I recognized all the work ahead to reestablish a life without her.

For years, I thought I had a close personal relationship with the being whom most call "God". Because of my sensitivity, and having had many transcendent experiences throughout my adult life, I believed one hundred percent that my children and I were "insiders," like a refined club in the heavens. Nothing terrible could happen to us. We were *special.* Now, as I looked around the almost soot-like room, I imagined something snickered at me. Was it a dark force laughing? "You lost yourself in the mind's trickery. Who do you think you are? We got her!"

The year before I also had a significant dream. I feared it had been a forewarning: Vast mountains surrounded me as I stood on a mountaintop. Within seconds, I descended thousands of miles. I kept thinking as I fell, *Oh, my God, Oh God, this is it … I'm going to die*!

Except my feet gracefully touched the ground. After awakening, I interpreted the vision to mean a tremendous experience was coming, more incomprehensible than anything I had ever known. Yet, the landing assured me that, even though all seemed lost during the descent, I would eventually be okay, and life would go on.

There *would* be a fall, but I would live. I assumed a global environmental disaster was on its way. Then my life went back into its routine. I shrugged the dream off, thinking maybe I'd get lucky and the disaster wouldn't occur. I never thought about that forewarning again.

My dream had come true. Charla's death was my fall from the mountain.

Losing her was incomprehensible, although I was grateful that Charla had come to me when I called for her. She was okay. But my mind would not stop tormenting itself. Could I have prevented her murder? Why hadn't I protected her more? I should have stayed married to her father. On and on, rough and reckless thoughts of guilt and shame bit into my heart.

The next morning, while showering, the same otherworldly green-blue light seeped around me. Charla! Even though there still weren't recognizable facial or body features, the shape and colors were the same. Emotionally unprepared for such a magnitude in the light of day, all I could do was look down at my feet and then up to the faucet. My embarrassed self challenged the embrace, as my naked body rejected her multidimensional visit. At the same time, my instincts wept somehow knowing this might be my last chance to connect with her in this form.

The encounter lasted for only seconds; then, her spirit dissolved away. I assumed she was moving onward from the earthly plane to express one last goodbye. After she disappeared, I sighed, thinking I'd been a fool. *Why hadn't I been more responsive?* Sometimes, we only have an instant to make an important decision that will affect us forever, but we don't realize it. Even though I'd had many experiences that had developed me, what still stuck with me was my childhood Christian foundation and shame at being naked. I wondered how long it would take me to stop regretting how I rejected her…

Once out of the shower and dressed, I grabbed my suitcase and with my purse over my shoulder, locked up my apartment. Driving to Marilyn's house was easier than I expected. As soon as I knocked on her front door, she greeted me with an embrace. "Soorya, I want you to know how much I love you and how sorry I am that this has happened."

"I love you too. So sorry for all of this." We held each other tightly.

As we caught the plane to Reno, Marilyn never complained about what she had to do to support me. We stayed silent, and I was grateful for that since I was a wrung-out washrag of remorse. I rubbed my hands together; they felt as numb as my guilt-ridden mind.

Detective Kim Garrett stood with a sign and we saw her as soon as we entered the terminal: late twenties, tall, blonde, and beautiful. I managed a smile. Not in uniform, Her bright purple blouse with matching sequins helped to lift my mood. Kim's calm demeanor caused me to burst into high-pitched chatter, spewing all my philosophies on what life could be in an ideal world with no violence. I embarrassed myself by how much I talked. Not the model of a grieving mother—whatever that model was.

"Soorya, I found a motel for you guys. We should drive over there and get you registered after you check in with the police and Social Services."

"Can we see Erika?"

"I'll call Joan about scheduling."

I nodded.

"Kim, I'm all over the place. One minute I feel light-headed and hyper. Then it's like I'm carrying bricks."

"I can't imagine what you are going through. We need to settle you so you can rest."

"Thank you. Yes, a wreck, that's me."

Kim's azure blue eyes pierced into me. She startled me by placing her hand over her heart, exactly as I had done the evening before, sitting next to the candle. I knew my situation had to be awkward for her. We were now a team and yet—we were two people who would always be chasms apart.

Chapter 4
Detectives

Inside the offices of the Washoe County Social Services Division, Marilyn and I perched on chairs facing someone's empty oak desk awaiting Kim, who had gone into a meeting. I yawned. Tossing and turning all night further marred my beat-up brain. I turned and focused on Marilyn's face. Red capillaries streaked the whites of her eyes. "Dear friend, how did you sleep?"

"I dozed here and there, but not much."

Just then, Kim tapped on the door. "The detectives will be here soon. I'll take you to another waiting room."

A knot hardened in my stomach, as I wasn't sure what came next. I wanted to wipe away all the bureaucracy and paperwork in my path. My most urgent concern was that Darren might kidnap my granddaughter Erika. I envisioned wrapping her inside a safety net and hiding her. Darren had killed my daughter, shot the judge presiding over their divorce case, and was now on the run. How could we not be terrified? I pressed my index finger into a fresh throbbing pain at the top of my left ribcage, working to release pressure, but it only seared worse.

A woman beckoned to us with her hand. "Please follow me."

As we passed different offices, I surmised that this section of the building wasn't accessible to the public. The architecture and decorum reflected homes in the 1950s. Everyone seemed laid back. We passed two women sharing cookies, and a third held a tin box offering more.

The environment comforted me. Each room had stories: photographs, quirky jokes, or inspiring posters. These individuals were strangers, yet I longed to be included in their tribe. My former life now destroyed, I was searching for solace and found a bit there. Someone had written in calligraphy: *It matters not who you love, where you love, why you love, when you love, or how you love. It matters only that you love. John Lennon.*

The quote brought another wave of anguish. My son-in-law did not understand how much Charla had surrendered to him throughout their marriage and how she'd suffered to please him.

My thoughts drifted back several years to an evening after Charla and Darren spent a weekend together at a workshop on relationships. I found my daughter sobbing uncontrollably on her bed. "I've done so many things wrong with Darren. I criticized him when I shouldn't have said anything. I feel awful that I've been hard on him."

Her remorse impressed me since I'd never seen her so upset. Charla was beside herself for weeks that she hadn't been a better wife.

Six months later, I visited Charla who was holding a bottle of wine in the kitchen.

"Remember when I was weeping in my bedroom after the workshop?"

"How could I forget?"

Charla snickered. "Well, I could have been kinder, true, but the fact is that no matter how many workshops I attend, no matter how accommodating I am, it will not fix our marriage. He wants things I can't give him. He's perverted."

Tears fell from Charla's eyes and she didn't bother to wipe them.

"Are you crying for Darren?"

"No, for myself and my disgusting predicament."

"Do you want to talk about it?"

"Not now. The less you learn, the better. Or you'll hate him."

That was the moment I learned my son-in-law had a darker character than I could have imagined.

Marilyn poked and startled me out of my daze. "Hey, can I get you anything?"

"No. Unless it's my former life."

"Right? It feels like we hopped on a freight train."

"And we haven't taken showers for a year."

Kim motioned for us to go down another hallway. She talked while we walked. "This process has been challenging for these men. They've been working around the clock with almost no rest."

A woman entered from behind. "Does anyone need food?"

"I'm starving," Marilyn answered.

"I'll pass." It almost seemed like a sacrilege to eat. The thought of Charla's suffering continued to drain away all gratifications.

Kim received a signal for us to meet the detectives. We entered what looked like a large cafeteria. Three men sat at a long wooden table with nineteenth-century style chairs.

Marilyn took a seat next to me. One detective, around thirty, with cropped light brown hair, nodded at me. Another with protruding muscles responded.

"Hello, Ms. Townley, my name is Ron Abramson." He turned to the man with a crew cut sitting next to him. "This is Detective Dave Garrison and Detective Jim Johnston." All had vivid blue eyes of varying shades.

Detective Abramson spoke. "We are here to answer any questions you have about your daughter or what is currently going on concerning Mr. Mack. We will be happy to inform you as far as we know."

None of the detectives reached over to shake my hand. Instead, they kept theirs folded on the table. Their humble stance reminded me of a solemn prayer position. They all wore regular cotton shirts, and each appeared around thirty. Detective Garrison said, "First, from all of us—we'd like to extend our condolences to you."

"Thank you," I said in a dull tone. "Yes, what happened is unthinkable." I couldn't organize better words.

These men seemed unusually stoic. They had worked with victims of heinous crimes before, were professionals, and gently waited for my responses. I imagined these brave souls had not hardened to the brutalities of life. Hopefully, they had families that brought them love. Like Kim, their softness put me at ease. "Pardon me, I'm feeling blank. Hold on for me to gather my thoughts."

"Certainly," one detective said. I would have bet money these men would have rather fixed an old rusted truck in the sweltering desert sun, over having to be here now, offering me gory details of my child's murder.

"First, I'd like to know about Judge Weller since he's still alive ..." I stammered.

Detective Johnston answered. "He's going to be fine. The bullet grazed his chest but didn't hit any internal organs. He required stitches, though, and hospitalization. We're happy to report he's on the mend."

"That's fantastic. I'm relieved to hear that."

Detective Garrison wove the story together. "What we know from the angle the bullets hit is that as soon as Judge Weller stood by a large window in his chambers, Mr. Mack or someone opened fire. The gentleman had to have known the judge's work schedule, and the exact time he would be in his chambers."

I looked at the detective, stunned, and thought how strange he called the shooter a "gentleman," but realized it must be routine for detectives to address suspects in a mannerly way.

"I heard his assistant, Annie Allison, was there as well—what happened to her?" I held my breath, thinking of yet another person traumatized.

"Ms. Allison first heard a loud shattering sound, then heard the judge scream for help."

Detective Garrison continued, "Ms. Allison ran toward Judge Weller to help him. She also got hit by some of the splintered fragments splaying around the room. She crawled to the front entrance and yelled into the hall for others to stay covered. As soon as the courthouse notified the police, we brought over our swat team. We combed the entire area."

I assumed Darren had kept firing shots. My voice shook. "Did anyone recognize the shooter?"

Detective Abramson held his finger up. "We have an eyewitness who saw a man with a rifle on the third floor of the parking unit facing directly across the courthouse and Judge Weller's office. Another witness said he'd heard an explosion while getting into his car."

"Are the windows of the judge's chambers positioned on the exact opposite side of the parking complex?"

"Yes. And the judge reported he had stood looking outside when the bullet hit him."

"It's summer, so the view was clear..."

My cheeks flushed. I remembered this sensation on my face once before, on a romantic date as a teen. But on this day, there was no excitement, only tripped electrical circuits across my entire nervous system. I took long breaths to stay present.

"Everything is still uncertain since we don't know where Mr. Mack is." Mr. Johnston said. "Our team has blocked off the entire area around the courthouse proper. Our unit had ordered employees to stay inside their buildings, but we finally let them out once we cleared the area."

The detective continued, "We closed down all businesses around the courthouse, as we don't know what Mr. Mack is planning."

They hadn't said anything about Charla.

Detective Garrison poured me a glass of water. "Ms. Townley, please take this."

"Thank you."

My mind drifted, imagining being on a strong tranquilizer. I bowed my head. After inhaling another long breath, I broke in.

"Who found my daughter?"

"Dave Jenkins, one of our detectives."

"Where are Charla's dogs?"

"They are at Joan Mack's house."

I took a breath, and appreciated Joan stepping forward.

Detective Abramson said. "Sparkles, Charla's dog, was in the car when we found her. She'd been in there for hours.

The garage was hot, so she got little oxygen. But luckily, she wasn't directly under the sun, and aside from dehydration and looking weak, she seems to be okay."

The detective looked away.

I emotionally fell to my knees and melted into a puddle. I couldn't fathom how vicious Darren had been. Sparkles had sat in that car, watching Charla being attacked by him and dying. Her mistress lay dying, but she couldn't reach her. Sparkles, a Lab, adored Charla. She followed her everywhere and offered constant kisses.

"Where is the cat, Tara?"

Tara had initially been mine; I had given her to Charla because I traveled too much for work, and Charla said she needed a mouser since they lived on several acres of land. "She's still at Mrs. Mack's rental house, and the landlord is feeding her."

"Was Charla shot?"

"No, she was attacked with a sharp object."

My eyes stay glued to the detective. "What time did all of this occur?"

"We have photos of Mrs. Mack driving into Mr. Mack's condo complex at 9:00 am. Our forensics expert determined she expired around 9:30 am."

Expired. Such a hollow word for death. If ever I'd felt the emptiness of everything, this was it.

When I was a child, my mother used to say that God never gives us more than we can handle. I didn't know if this was true. But in some vague way, watching all three strong men with their slumped shoulders helped me to endure the first details about Charla's death. Here before me were the heroes who fought for justice and kept our society stable. They were a comforting, stabilizing contrast to the devastation in my heart.

Just then, a new woman came in and whispered something to one detective.

"Ms. Townley, we have a lead on Darren, and have to go. Do you have any more questions?"

"You've given me a lot. Thank you for meeting with me today."

Detective Abramson said, "Again, we are very sorry for your loss and everything else you and your family are going through."

I leaned forward and shook each of the men's hands. It felt nourishing to touch them. "I appreciate all your efforts and how much extra work this is causing you." I imagined that for every murderer like Darren, there were many more men like these in the world, men who protect life instead of destroying it.

My head turned to Marilyn. It surprised me she'd had her arm tightly wrapped around my shoulders the entire time. I hadn't felt her presence in that room until then.

At the motel, as Marilyn took a short nap, I went out and got a newspaper from the front office. It reported that Charla had been attacked with a hunting knife. I knew the detectives had wanted to be gentle with me. They never used the word blade. They'd spared me the gruesome details of the murder scene that they had to personally confront. While I was grateful for the information they gave me, I needed to know more.

Did she suffer, or was it quick, like the detective said?

Were her last breaths agonizingly long? Did she panic about Erika?

Chapter 5
Social Services

By now, I'd memorized the walk to the Social Service Division. A middle-aged woman named Diane Wozinack waited for us behind a large wooden desk, papers divided into even patterned rows. I'd eaten nothing but a banana since I got the news two days prior.

Diane stood and reached out her hand. "I am very sorry for the loss of your daughter. There are no words to express my sadness." Diane's voice grew firmer. "I've learned that you want custody of your granddaughter."

"Yes, and my daughter desired that as well."

Diane motioned for us to the seats in front of her desk. "Please sit. As you probably know, Joan Mack already has temporary guardianship of Erika."

My face grimaced. "I don't understand how this occurred so fast. No one informed me."

"You were in California, and Charla's father didn't volunteer. Joan immediately filed for custody and the presiding judge granted it."

A gust of angst rushed through me. I yearned to leap out of my chair and save my granddaughter.

"To get permanent custody, you'll have to move to Reno, establish residency, and then take classes to be licensed by the State of Nevada. It's a formal procedure that every applicant completes. At this stage, you'll be placed in the Foster Parent category, even though, in reality you are Erika's grandmother, like Joan. But first, you two need an FBI clearance. Both of you must attend the same classes and go through the exact procedures."

My ears listened to Diane's instructions, but inside I was a growling animal spreading its claws through the bars of a cage.

I asked, "So, the State of Nevada has official custody of Erika, but Joan has temporary custody?"

Diane kept her tone level. "Yes, Erika is under what's called an Emergency Order."

Flabbergasted, I silently questioned the process. *Why has our society become such a machine? Why is everything so complicated? I'm standing here 24 hours after my daughter died, and it still wasn't fast enough to get custody of my granddaughter!*

But then I realized the logic. The state of Nevada had moved to protect a vulnerable child. At least they hadn't assigned her to a foster home, and Joan loved her, but ...

"Is this because Charla didn't leave a will? She told several of her girlfriends, and me many times, that she wanted me to raise Erika if anything happened to her."

"Unfortunately, she didn't leave that in writing, so it's just hearsay. Every procedure toward obtaining custody must go through proper legal channels. I strongly suggest you hire a lawyer as soon as possible."

My empty stomach cringed. I had to act fast.

"You could get the ball rolling on an FBI clearance within a day or so."

"No problem, I'll get on it."

The clock glared past 1:00 pm, and I still hadn't even seen Erika. Time had never been as important to me.

Marilyn asked, "Diane, could you tell how Erika was doing when you saw her?"

"The police kept her at the station for over eight hours until midnight. She must have been exhausted, and surely, she sensed something awful had occurred. The other two grandparents, Mr. Sampsel and Mrs. Mack, came in and told her about her mother. I heard she sobbed afterward. Then they took her to Mrs. Mack's house."

I bit my lip. When I looked up, Diane appeared downcast as well. Her mouth tightened.

"I can't wait to see her."

"I can only imagine. Good luck with everything you need to get done."

The room began spinning like I had vertigo. "Are you okay? Would you like some water?" Marilyn asked.

"I'll get a cup of water," Diane said.

"No, thank you both. There's too much happening. It's not about needing water. I think I'd like to take a quick nap before seeing Erika."

As Marilyn and I waited outside for Kim to bring the car, Joan Mack stood ahead of us at the front of the Police Station. She startled me by being there. Joan looked our way but made no gesture to acknowledge us. Marilyn and I approached her. I couldn't switch emotional gears and say much to her. I resented that she hadn't waited to spill the dreadful news to Erika. I would have thought maybe they could have said Charla was sick for a while then told her. We three grandparents could have talked it through and decided together. My nerves spun, similar to spiders fleeing a crash.

Joan held a steady stare at us. Since she said nothing, it felt creepy. Her disheveled clothes and tangled hair appeared dirty. I'd forgotten how short she was. I assumed she was just as surprised to see me as I was her.

"I'm here on business."

Joan's first words to me were a bitter disappointment. If a two-headed serpent and the bride of Godzilla were joined at the altar speaking vows, I would have equated that with her utterance, considering her son had just slaughtered my daughter.

Even though she let me down, I reached out to hug her. In a slight movement, she turned her upper body, and my embrace didn't land right. Then she pushed me away with one hand. No one would have seen her subtle gesture. *She's not embracing me. It's the contrary. I thought she'd at least give me her condolences.*

"Hi, Joan." I forced myself to sound normal. "This is my friend Marilyn."

"Hello." Joan never looked at either of us.

"Hi, nice to meet you." Marilyn didn't reach out her hand.

Greeting robots would have done a better job. I fought back my feelings.

Joan was an ice cube and I was a glob of shock. My physical embrace with her left me even more adrift. I'd massaged this woman for a decade. We had conversations about life, philosophy, and spirituality on the phone. We'd spent Christmas dinners together. Why weren't we sobbing in each other's arms? Why weren't we letting down with each other—two mothers engulfed in this tragedy? We should have shared our mutual grief.

On a foolish impulse, I walked behind her and rubbed her shoulders as I had habitually done throughout the years. It had been my place, the server. She'd always loved my touch and would moan with pleasure. Now, my all-thumbs gesture gave her the upper hand, literally, by me pining for affection. But habits are hard to break. Even though I embarrassed myself, I knew Joan was suffering as well. I empathized with her.

Throughout the decade, I knew her up to a point, but Joan always seemed unapproachable for authentic intimacy. Now, she was even harder to read. It was apparent she was not driving in my direction on the emotional highway. She'd just steered herself away and onto a back road.

I kept seeing more extreme polarities in front of me: the mother of the killer versus the mother of the victim. But what unsettled me most was that she wasn't showing any empathy for what I was going through on any level and she hadn't been thoughtful enough to wait until I was present to tell Erika what had happened.

If I'd sunk into the bowels of the earth, I would have dug further working to find Joan's authentic self. But for now, at least I felt compassion for her.

Joan had been through hell already in her past. When she turned fifty, a plane crash killed her husband, Dennis Alan Makovsky (who changed his last name to Mack before Darren was born). Dennis was returning from a jewelry-buying trip and flew his private plane back to Reno. The airport had cleared his plane's route for landing, but it got caught in a jet wash from an airliner and crashed. He died instantly.

Joan shared with me one day that she was "incapacitated" after Dennis's death. The family stayed with her day and night for a long time. "I depended on Darren the most," she said.

Darren was also given the macabre task of sorting through the plane wreckage to recover the jewels that Dennis was carrying with him when his plane crashed. Darren would confide to family members years later that the experience had scarred him, as there were bits of his dad's flesh spread across the crash site, but he had to recover the jewelry at his mother's insistence.

After her husband's tragic death, Joan gave Darren, who was then twenty-four, fifty percent ownership of Palace Jewelry and Loan, the largest pawn shop in the state of Nevada, located in a prime location just under the massive, always-lit sign straddling Virginia boulevard, "Reno: The Biggest Little City in the World." Darren immediately took over as manager so Joan could grieve.

Ultimately, Darren won full control over Palace Jewelry and Loan. In the process, he became a multimillionaire, making at one point $44,000 a month. When Charla met him in 1993, fresh from his first divorce, and already the father of two children, he was driving a red Ferrari. But Darren had novel business ideas, which created conflict with Joan. He would say his mother was "outdated" and "old fashioned" and that she would undermine his authority with their employees.

The December before Charla was murdered I had visited her. We built a roaring fire inside her fireplace and drank tea while being philosophical about what went wrong with her and Darren's relationship: "A red flag when I first flew to Reno and had barely known him was that he rushed out of a meeting at the store saying, 'She's a fucking cunt.' This was his mother. I was shocked but so enthralled with him I ignored the sign that something might be wrong with him."

Now here I was dealing with Joan and imagined she must have felt remorse or guilt about what Darren had done. Surely a mother, any mother, suffers when their child commits a crime, and parents almost always bear some blame for our children's misdeeds. She had to be shaken and in shock, like me.

And I was now holding the mirror, showing her Darren as, at least in part, a reflection of her. I wondered, had Joan ever really loved Charla?

Kim drove up and parked along the curb. Joan half-looked her way. Kim got out of the car and came over. "Hello, Joan. It's nice to see you again."

Joan said nothing.

"We have to get going," I said to Joan, who still wouldn't look at me. "I'll call you as soon as I get free to come and see Erika."

"Just let me know first because we could be out."

"Where's Erika right now?"

"Lanny's taking care of her."

I didn't reach out physically this time. Joan turned and walked away. In the car, Kim said, "I registered you under a pseudonym."

"I like that."

"I'm sure that encounter was stressful on you. I didn't know she'd be here."

"Stressful doesn't even touch it."

Our motel room faced the noisy side of the freeway, but I couldn't wait to plop down on the bed.

Two hours later, Kim picked us up again, and we drove to a toy store.

I realized right away that the coloring books were too immature for an eight-year-old. I bought three boxes of puzzles. "This will keep us working together as a family," I said to Marilyn.

We informed Joan we were on our way. I was beyond excited (and apprehensive) to see Erika. Once on Joan's front porch, she opened the door on the first knock. She had the same clothes on, looking like she'd slept in them like me, but now her lipstick smeared upward like a happy but hidden clown. Her demeanor exceeded my expectations. "Hello, come on in." She even smiled.

Lanny, Darren's younger brother, was seated at the dining room table, and looked up. He didn't stand to greet us and was quietly weeping. I'd been around Lanny for many years, but never had any meaningful connection with him. For the first time, I saw he had a tender heart, a heart that could mourn.

I raised my voice since the guy couldn't or wouldn't get up and walk over to us. "Lanny," I said loudly, "this is my friend, Marilyn, from Los Angeles."

"Hello, Marilyn, from Los Angeles." Lanny hadn't lost his wit, but now it was out of place.

I was surprised that he could joke. Tears continued to stream down Lanny's face. Everything felt indelicate and unmanageable. No one invited us to sit or to have a cup of tea. Joan finally spoke. "I'll go see where Erika is." She left the room.

Charla's dogs, Sparkles and Charla's other dog, Licorice raced in, lifting the tension. Sparkles jumped on me and licked my arm. She used to annoy me with her saliva. Now, her affection was refreshing. I rubbed her ears and thanked her, then placed my arms and chest on top of her. "Sweetheart I know. You lost your life like us."

Sparkles. My God, I had so much compassion for her. She was a victim, too. Licorice came over, panting, and jumping wildly. She was an inbred Labrador, and I didn't think the transition to a new owner upset her. I just kept thinking: *Sparkles had witnessed and endured all of it. Every knife thrust.*

Joan opened the door. "Erika's outside."

"I'm thankful you are giving a home to the dogs because trying to find a rental with them would be daunting. You could have sent them to the pound."

"Oh, I would *never* do that," Joan said in a determined voice.

"Well, I'm relieved you are generous enough to help them."

Joan lifted her head a little as if in agreement, then went into the kitchen. Everything had radically changed for us all, and like a slap on the face, here we were. But I couldn't grieve any longer over the dogs. Marilyn and I gave each other 'the look' to go outside.

"Hi, sweetheart. I'm so happy to see you!"

"Hi, Grandma. It's nice to see you too."

Erika didn't walk closer for a hug, and I froze, too.

"This is my good friend Marilyn from LA. She lives near me there. We are like sisters."

"Hi, Marilyn."

I wanted to hold her until we felt united.

My darling granddaughter held a basketball as she stood erect. Her voice was without enthusiasm, and her droopy eyes said it all. I walked closer, and she responded by leaning in and extending her hand.

"Can I have the ball? I'll try to make a basket."

Inside, I exploded with anxiety. I wanted to fix our feelings, but we had become characters in a horror movie and couldn't escape the peculiar production.

Erika broke the spell and tossed it to me, but I missed.

"Gosh, I'm out of it."

For a long minute, we took turns missing and finally, making the hoop. Marilyn said, "I'm going into the house to let you guys have some private time."

Erika opened up the second she left. "I just can't believe it, Grandma."

"I know, honey; I can't believe it either. So, so sorry."

Something in me broke even more. I didn't know how to behave or what to say—not knowing whether to reach out and touch Erika tenderly, or wait for her to reach out to me. I couldn't read her. I was afraid any gesture might overwhelm her. *I must wait for this little girl to come to me. What she is going through and enduring is unimaginable.*

"This is such a hard experience for you, but I want you to know I love you very, very much and I am here for you in every way."

Erika remained silent, but moved closer, reached out within seconds, hugged me warmly. She only talked about the dogs. Erika picked up a small ball lying near the edge of the patio and tossed it to them. We went through the motions of playing. Those moments were a kind of grace. It helped us to clear our heads by exercising our muscles. If I weren't there with Erika, I would have been curled up in the motel bed. My heart bled for this child. I was present at the moment of her birth. Because she'd had the umbilical cord wrapped around her neck, the doctor took her away, and I stood next to him and was the first person in our family to touch her. It had felt significant and like an honor. My memories were too massive for me to bear. I had to let all thinking go away for a while.

"How are Uncle Christopher and Aunt Genicia?"

"They're fine, honey. They'll be here tomorrow. It's a long flight from India."

Erika gave a thumbs up. Charla's devotion to her daughter showed. Erika was smart, and always asked bright questions. Charla had read to her nightly and had kept her engaged with interesting art projects.

Now we were broken.

Marilyn brought us icy glasses of lemonade. Afterward we walked to the Truckee River, next to Joan's property. Birds flew above us and then landed on the water, cleaning their wings. We began picking up stones and throwing them into the river, watching them splash in circles. Each time I threw a rock, I thought of yet another person who would be crushed by Charla's death. Then I reminded myself that Erika was the most crushed of all.

Being next to the flowing water offered a kind of healing balm, as if Mother Nature was soothing us—or at least me.

I could tell by Marilyn's trembling chin that she was breaking down as she stood in the sand. She was a mother with a daughter and a son.

Yet for me, holding those rocks brought something back to life. I felt a sense of strength from the earth. The river soothed and seemed to say, *you are the one who needs the most nurturing right now to pull yourself together so you can help this damaged little girl.*

I tossed a stone into the water. The tide promised it would soon flow differently. Reno is a windy city, and a breeze usually arrives. That day, it refreshed my skin as my bare feet stood in the water, while nature pulled along its natural journey, all my thoughts subsided as the ripples neared my feet. In the heat of the June weather, the fresh coolness was my first respite.

Chapter 6
America's Most Wanted

Marilyn walked over to me and interrupted my brief moment with Erika beside the river. "Let's go. You're supposed to meet Diane."

"Right."

I kneeled to the water, dug into the soggy dirt and squeezed my hands. Even though the soil had felt regenerating, as soon as I shook off the mud and walked toward the house, the familiar brain fog bewilderment I'd gone through in my apartment returned.

For years, I had practiced mindful awareness, which always began before dawn with a daily ritual of observing the sun rising over the mountains. It was a time for me to offer a prayer of peace for the world. Now, that routine was no more. My inspiration died along with my daughter.

As I walked toward Joan's house, I glanced back at the river, continuing its journey. Gold flickered into shades of blue as the sunlight burst and paraded along the surface of the stream. Nature had not diminished my sorrow, but it had given me strength.

Lanny still sat in the same spot as before. Joan was a few feet away in the kitchen, preparing food. I said out loud, "I have an appointment. Marilyn and I will be back later if that works with your schedule. I'd like to spend more time with Erika."

"That's fine. I'm sure she'll enjoy the company. Drive safely."

Joan smiled. In the past, she had always used appropriate social graces. Her former personality had made me believe she was a kind person.

But she still hasn't asked me how I'm feeling or how my family is doing. It's like we've been through nothing to her.

Just then, Erika entered from the back door of the kitchen. "Honey, I have an appointment. But I'll come back soon."

"Okay. Bye, Grandma. See you later."

Erika's tone sounded lighter; I was grateful we'd experienced the river together. She also seemed content to stay at Joan's for now. She was holding some drawing paper. I shrugged off my fear of Darren kidnapping her. *How would Joan handle it if that occurred?*

My granddaughter and I hugged again, and it relieved me.

I filled out some forms at the Social Service office, and then we drove back to see Erika. I'd never been at ease at Joan's house and felt even more put off now. The dim entrance featured a display of large family photographs including Joan's parents, pictures of Charla with Darren, and all the children together.

There was no way one could avoid the faces lining the walls. I wondered what it was like for Erika to see her smiling mother each time she walked through that hall. I approached Joan. "Do you think these pictures of Charla might re-traumatize Erika? What do you think about taking them down for a while?"

Joan looked me up and down with wide eyes. Her lips twisted. "I'm *sure* she's fine with it."

No room for my consideration. She had brushed me off. But I didn't want to insist since she had full custody. If I gave her grief, she might forbid me from taking Erika for sleepovers. I was on a wobbling edge, holding on tightly, so I stayed silent. Each time I used the toilet, I had to pass by Erika's smiling mother, on the wall next to multiple photos of her murderous husband. I continued to worry about Erika's trauma. I kept thinking: how could Joan be so out of touch with human emotions that she didn't even consider Erika's?

In the large, dimly-lit, wood paneled, sprawling house, I didn't know where Erika was, so I went next to a window and saw Kim and Joan talking outside. Erika was with them by the basketball hoop again. I realized Lanny had left; I didn't know where Marilyn was; the house was quiet. I convinced myself we were all in such confused emotional states, we just kept wandering around, feeling tenuous, moving here and there.

Since Kim and Joan engaged in conversation, I thought I was alone until I realized Darren's first cousin, Corey Schmidt, who lived directly across from Darren at the Fleur de Lis complex was standing next to me. He was the guy who called Charla late one night, drunk, telling her he wanted to make love to her. Charla had laughed it off one day on the phone. "Corey and Darren are super tight, and Joan begged Corey to come work at the Palace."

I had asked, "Why did you take his advances so lightly?"

"Well, he was drunk. And lonely."

"Do they ever call their business a pawnshop?"

"Rarely. It's always the *Palace.*" Charla had chuckled.

The *Reno Gazette-Journal* reported that Corey spoke to Darren within minutes of Darren ambushing Charla.

Glancing at Corey now, I wished he would have been there. She might have survived.

It felt appropriate that I waited for Corey to speak first. His stick-figure posture stood immobile. *Oh my God, he won't say anything. He will not acknowledge me, positive or negative.* I stayed still, waiting. Waiting for him to express something, anything. His behavior was yet another rude awakening. My stark and dismal future with this family was as awful as if I had torn skin off my body.

Even if my family was upset with you, they'd still acknowledge you, most likely sarcastically, but they'd treat you like you existed. Mack's family's way of dealing with horrible experiences was to dismiss them—and I feared such behavior might affect Erika. I didn't want them to misarrange her emotions so that she was forced to suppress anything.

Every time I opened my mouth to communicate with Corey, something stopped me.

Joan, Marilyn, and Kim joined us. I silently screamed, "Thank God, you're back!" By now, Corey and I had sat silently together in the same room for over fifteen minutes.

I grabbed Marilyn's hand and whispered, "Can we talk in private?"

"Sure, let's take a walk."

Outside, I let loose. "This situation is too big for me. I'm choosing to leave Erika here."

"I think that's wise."

Back in the house, I embraced Erika. Marilyn asked for a hug, and she gave her one.

As I gathered my things, I was so unnerved by Corey still sitting in the same spot in such a deadpan manner that I tripped and spilled my purse on to the floor. Marilyn kneeled to help me pick everything up.

Erika came in behind us. "Bye, Grandma. See you tomorrow."

"Yes, sweetheart, you will, and I'll bring Christopher and Genicia next time."

"I'm so glad." She reached out and hugged me for the third time. Joan walked over. "Let me walk you to the door."

Joan surprised me by opening her arms and hugging. Again, though, she did that same half-turn, avoiding contact. I knew it was just a show for Kim.

In the car, I said to Kim, "I wanted to take Erika, but I was afraid she would be bored."

"I completely understand. It's hard to entertain children when there are so many loose ends to manage. At the motel, there would be nothing for her to do except be stuck in front of a television."

Marilyn leaned forward from the back seat and placed her hand on my shoulder.

"Be pragmatic this week, dear friend. Erika will be better off with you when things are more settled."

"I agree with Marilyn. Give yourself a few days."

That night in our room, Marilyn and I stayed up late talking. My cell rang nonstop for hours: Clients, friends, and media calls would not stop. I repeated what I knew. My ears hurt from pressing the phone into them. But I was afraid of missing a call from my son, so I left it on.

"Marilyn, I can't believe that I actually rubbed Joan's shoulder's today. I felt like a fool."

"You're in shock. You got nervous."

It was only 8:00 pm, but I was fading. "Can we go to sleep?"

"Absolutely. We'll get some real rest tonight since it's so early."

Right away, I fell into a dream:

I was inside pieces of a moving structure in a seascape. Seashells, and creatures roamed as if they were cartoon characters. When I touched the scene, it felt dirty, and every movement was filmy and hazy. I tripped over slimy rocks while large fish almost smashed into me, but then slipped away in another direction. As I stumbled along, it felt disorderly, but I didn't know why. I recognized it wasn't because I was afraid. Instead, just sadness. I was a creature saturated in sorrow. I had a big "aha" moment, bringing understanding. Yet when I awoke, I couldn't remember what that big "aha" was. The dream had reminded me, though, of when I was at Joan's house when we were all like fish roaming around doing nothing.

At 10:30 pm, Kim woke us with a call.

"Fred Peabody from the Fox television show *America's Most Wanted* is flying in. He wants to interview you on camera. He's requesting that you plead for Darren to turn himself in. Fred wants to know if he can have your cell number?"

"That would be great." My voice sounded small. I was nervous, but I wanted Darren to hear my plea.

"I'll call him. See you tomorrow."

By early morning, Fred Peabody waited for me in an immense room at the police department set up with equipment and lighting. A crew member fitted me with a microphone.

Fred introduced himself first. "The crew is ready any time you are, Soorya."

Facing the camera, Fred told the story and then introduced me.

I imagined Darren was near a television, listening. "Darren, your actions have *devastated* our families. Please turn yourself in."

I used my belly for a guttural, distinctive tone on the word, devastated. Fred asked, "Do you hate Darren?"

"No, he's my son-in-law, and love is the greatest force there is." The room stilled. One cameraman rubbed his eyes.

Fred said quietly, "You're right, and this kind of reasoning is the way it should ultimately be for everyone."

Once finished, the same crew person came up to me. "That was remarkable what you said."

"My entire life has been about generating love. I can't stop now."

We had been an actual family, and like a wilted flower, some of the scent still lingered inside me.

I was grateful to be around media people, to whom I didn't have to explain my story from scratch. They knew more than I did. Despite it all, I was more fortunate than many parents who never found their child's killer. To express that I felt grateful would have sounded odd. But there it was: my family and I were luckier than many who lose loved ones.

That afternoon, I met my son Christopher and his wife Genicia at the Reno International Airport. They were exhausted from an inter-continental flight but ready to help us in whatever way they could.

Arriving at the Washoe County Social Services office, Kim and Diane Wozniak introduced themselves to Christopher and Genicia. Diane said, "This is abrupt after just coming in from overseas, but you and Genicia have to get an FBI clearance for Erika to stay in the same house with you, just like Soorya."

Kim said, "Christopher, I'm officially handing over the car keys to you so you can drive now."

"Great. It will give us the freedom not to burden you every time we need something."

"You could never be a burden, Christopher, but I know what you mean."

As much as I dreaded going back that afternoon, I shook away the repulsion while Christopher, Genicia, Marilyn, and I stood on Joan's front porch pensively waiting for the door to open. She graciously greeted us, but it felt like a massive machine started sucking away the tiny renewed energy I had gained from the river the day before and from uniting with my family. Maybe it was because I could feel Christopher's rage. Maybe because I wasn't in touch with my own. "Hello everyone, hello ..." Joan greeted, in her pawn shop velvet-like twang.

"Joan, this is Genicia, Christopher's wife. You've met her before at ... gatherings." I almost said, "At Charla's," but caught myself.

"Yes, I remember. Come in, please. Erika's outside."

Lanny was back in his spot behind the dining table. He didn't get up to greet Christopher, who squinted his eyes at Joan and snorted some sound loudly through his mouth, completely ignoring Lanny. Joan hurried over and whispered in my ear, "Wow, Christopher sure is angry."

"He has a lot to be angry about." I glared at her with damaging eyes.

I couldn't tell if Christopher had heard our conversation. Just then, Erika burst through.

"Hello!" she bellowed.

"Aunt Ha-knee-c-a, Uncle Christopher!" Erika was so sweet the way she properly pronounced Geni's name. She took turns flying into both of their arms. For the first time, I felt the warmth of family.

Charla had always called her home the "Fun House" for children. Whenever Christopher showed up, especially in the winter, he had been the "fun uncle" who played with the kids. They also made snowmen and rode sleds. It had been a tiny break for Charla as she and I would sit to the side on rocks sipping hot tea gossiping or gabbing and catching up.

Joan approached closer. "I'm going upstairs to leave you guys alone." Poor Joan. I felt sorry for her now.

Erika led us to the cavernous family den, which was filled with all kinds of board games. The room had the same dark brown paneling as the rest of the house. An elaborate chess set made from ivory sat on a center table. We chose Chutes and Ladders because we didn't have to think. Marilyn said, "You guys play since there are four of you."

Marilyn paced the room. Something agitated her. She settled underneath the head of one of Dennis Mack's hanging hunting trophies, a mounted moose. Then she came and kneeled beside me. "Now that Chris and Geni are here, I'm flying back on standby tonight."

"Oh, Marilyn, I don't want you to go."

"I know, honey, although you'll settle into new routines, and you guys now have each other."

Marilyn had been my anchor. But she had a life.

"I'm going to call the airline. Be right back."

We'd been in the dark den for two hours. I could tell Christopher felt beyond annoyed because it was where Darren grew up as a child.

"Mom, I can't take it any longer," he gritted his teeth while whispering so Erika and Geni, engaged in conversation, couldn't hear.

As soon as Marilyn came back with a thumbs up, Christopher said, "Let's get out of here."

The hardest part was leaving Erika. Again. This time, it felt selfish to not bring her with us.

Amid all the murkiness, we managed pleasant goodbyes—or at least Joan, Geni, and I did. Lanny remained sitting, not reaching out in any way, and my son refused to acknowledge either of them. "Honey, we'll be back as soon as possible,"

I stroked Erika's hair. This sweet child reached out and clung to Geni. They had been close from the beginning.

As we drove to the airport, Christopher said, "I had a sick feeling while at that house. I believe it's partly Joan's fault for what he did."

"I see your point. But Joan is suffering too and going through hell like us. Right now, she's just a mother. Let's not be harsh with her while she doesn't even know where Darren is."

"I'm not sure if I can do that. I'm too infuriated."

"I get it. I truly do."

The intense summer heat penetrated the car. And the fury of Christopher's rage made it worse. I was grateful Erika wasn't with us because of the tension. Everything felt like thick, slippery glass cracking underneath us, and there was nothing to be done about it.

At the airport, we all expressed loving farewells. Christopher spoke first. "Marilyn, I can't thank you enough for all your help. You've been such a solid friend and so kind to my mother."

"Oh, Christopher, I would do anything for your mom." Marilyn wiped her eyes.

I kissed her on the cheek and my arms didn't want to let her go.

We watched her plane fly away in silence. Afterward, all I could think of was going to Jamba Juice to get a fresh crushed ice orange drink. I felt guilty, though, like somehow, I was betraying Charla by craving a sensory gratification. All I had eaten since the murder was two bananas and that was to placate Kim and Marilyn, who worried about me. And yet, now I suddenly craved a slushy drink.

Christopher snapped me back to reality. "Mom, you need to find a lawyer as soon as possible."

Geni and I looked at each other with wide eyes, mine in a panic. "Where do we start?" I asked.

"We'll figure it out," Christopher said.

We still hadn't been to the morgue.

Chapter 7
Lawyers

June 15, 2006

We hadn't intended to hunker down in a sweltering car smack in the middle of summer. But a restaurant server had given us the stink eye to move on.

The auto air conditioner couldn't keep up. Sweat beads moistened our faces as we sped through lists of lawyers recommended by friends and my LA clients. We cold-called everyone who knew anyone who might help. "I'm tired. Are you guys wiped out too?"

"Yea, but more because we can't find anyone." Geni sighed.

Each time we spoke to another lawyer, that person declared the same thing. *Mr. Darren Mack or his family had previously hired us. Thus, by Nevada law, taking you on as a client would be an infraction, a conflict of interest.* One lawyer finally admitted, "Every lawyer in Reno knows that the Macks pay lawyers their initial fee so that others can't use them for a lawsuit. Please don't mention my name. If you repeat what I said, I'll deny it."

Another: "I wouldn't touch a case involving that family with a twelve-foot pole; they fight too dirty."

Cramped in the car, the three of us kept taking deep breaths and gulping down warm bottled water. We drove to an appointment with a family law attorney who sounded promising. He escorted us to sit on his plush leather furniture. He began: "I want you to understand up front, I'm expensive. This case is intricate, and you'll have to be prepared to lay out a lot of cash."

After mentioning the intended colossal chunk of change four times, never narrowing it down to an actual amount, we three darted looks onto each other and motioned subtly toward the door. While the guy kept talking and walking around the room, we stood and politely thanked him for his time.

All the responses from prospective lawyers felt like my sweat—annoying and unpleasant. One time when Charla went on a diatribe about her impending divorce. I responded with positive spiritual counsel. She retorted, "You can't understand because you're an innocent."

I brushed off her comment, thinking she was paranoid and being negative. After all, I had lived most of my life in California—the hub of new-age positive thinking. Now, I understood part of what she had endured with the Mack family. Not only was there incredible stress just to pick legal counsel, but then we'd have to fork out the fees.

Christopher looked out the car window. "Mom, this is hard. I don't feel desperate yet, but I'm wondering what will we do if we can't find someone local?"

His voice trailed off. Genicia nudged him. I knew she didn't want me any more paranoid than I was. "Where do we go from here?" I asked. "Should I call around in Las Vegas?"

My voice hesitated. "Because that would mean I'll be paying for their plane flights, hotels, and food expenses each time there's a custody hearing."

I envisioned a pitiful credit score.

"Let's have faith we can stay in Reno," Genicia said in the most serious voice I'd ever heard from her. We sat motionless.

The shadow of a tree branch fell over our windshield. The sun was setting. We had lost another day. Inside of me there was a solemn contemplation, feeling bewildered.

"I've got to go to the john, and then we *have* to get out of this car," Christopher moaned.

As soon as he left, my cell rang. It was Shawn Meador, Charla's former lawyer. "Soorya, I think I've found someone for you. His name is Egan Walker. Egan worked for the Sheriff's Department for fifteen years, and besides being a hell of a guy, he's a smart and hardworking lawyer. Best of all, though, he has integrity—I know you'll like him."

After we hung up, I could hardly contain myself. I wanted to jump hopscotch in the street.

I imagined attorneys calling each other, especially when a sensational murder case rocked the city. "Words move around like fireflies. Someone let Shawn know we needed help."

I quickly called the number on speakerphone. "Mr. Walker?"

"Yes, this is him."

Geni crossed two fingers on one hand and her eyes pierced into mine. It surprised me he answered on the first ring.

"My name is Soorya Townley, and Shawn Meador gave me your number."

"Hello Soorya, Shawn informed me you need help. Let's set up an appointment immediately."

When Christopher came back, I was close to shouting. "You won't believe this—but in the time you were gone, Shawn Meador found us a local lawyer!"

"That's incredible, Mom. When are you meeting that person?"

"Tomorrow morning. Let's celebrate tonight and get some snacks. I'll even eat some food!" We all laughed. Suddenly, I was ravenous.

♦

Mr. Walker's office was in central Reno, in an unpretentious two-story building. Photos along the walls displayed his five children. On his desk, next to his computer, was a large photo of a smiling, light-haired, beautiful woman. "That's my wife, Shelley."

Egan had piercing, stunning blue eyes and a military-grade crew cut. His stocky build made me feel protected. He motioned for us to sit in front of his desk "First, I want to express how deeply sorry I am for the loss of your daughter. I can't even imagine what you are going through right now as a mother, Soorya, and for you, Christopher, as Charla's brother. Also, for your entire family."

Mr. Walker continued. "A criminal murdered my best friend five years ago, and losing him has been one of the most devastating experiences of my life. He was a police officer, and it happened on the job. Some guy just randomly walked up and outright shot him." His face turned toward the wall.

Was it providence? This man and I, perhaps through our mutual sorrow, had found each other. He was the perfect fit. And not because I was desperate. It was Mr. Walker's demeanor, words, and the way his eyes revealed depths of compassion. I felt divinity coming through again to help us. There was no doubt.

Mr. Walker laid out a plan. "First, I want to study Darren and Charla's court proceedings to see what occurred with Judge Weller. I also want to get you more rights with Erika."

As this man spoke, I realized how awkward a murder situation is for everyone. How does a compassionate person talk to a victim? How does a victim respond? It felt like grabbing a metal pole with bare hands during a blizzard. Social graces and proper responses would never be enough to make anyone feel comfortable.

"Mr. Walker …"

"Please—call me Egan. All my friends do."

"Egan. Thank you so much for everything you are about to do. Your presence gives me solace from these horrendous last few days."

"I appreciate that, Soorya, and it's my honor to assist you and your family. You've been through a tremendous experience, and I want to make life as easy as possible for you during this time."

After Egan left the room, we took a vote, and all gave an enthusiastic "Yes!"

Mr. Walker returned with three cups of water. As he approached me, I realized my T-shirt was dirty—I had dripped toothpaste on it. Christopher and Genicia were shaggy-looking, too. Thankfully, Egan didn't seem to notice. "Here you are. Be careful, it's full"

Egan moved on to more immediate issues. "I don't know what Joan and Lanny are up to, but I want to have everything necessary filed, just in case they come at you suddenly through a specific custody motion."

As Egan's words rang out, I still clung to hope, though, that Joan knew from our decade together that I was serious about raising Erika, and I hoped her being rational would rule and she wouldn't resist my efforts to have primary custody. Besides, I was ten years younger than her!

In my world, common sense screamed I should have my daughter's child.

"As you know, Soorya, the courts had to place Erika with Joan since Darren is out of the picture. The reason they didn't consider you is that you weren't here. It's imperative now that you move to Reno as quickly as possible to establish residency if you really want custody."

"Yes, Social Services warned me several times that I have to do everything as fast as possible. Christopher, Genicia and I are planning to fly back to LA to move my things. I've already quit my LA job."

Without a lawyer, it had been impossible to know what actions to take next, and with Social Services, I wanted to sound like I had a tight plan, which I didn't have. Egan Walker had just saved my life.

"You are doing an amazing job, Soorya, holding it all together."

"Thank you. I'm grateful for your thoughts."

Egan stood and leaned over his desk as if looking for a paper. "Soorya, this is a tough question for me to ask. I know how hard it is to raise a child. I have five. I'm not sure I would be up for taking on another at my age, and I'm only in my early forties. Are you absolutely one hundred percent certain you want to do this? Are you sure you want to raise Erika when you are almost sixty years old? You realize it's becoming a mother all over again ..."

Egan held his piercing gaze on me like a magnifying glass. He needed me to be strong enough to carry the weight to endure whatever court battle required.

"No matter what I have to do, no matter what it takes, I'll walk through the fires of hell if I have to. This is the least I can do for my daughter."

My hollow body was numb again. But my head no longer hazed—there was a new clarity. A bucket of tears erupted, pouring down my face for the first time—finally!

I'd meant my words. But they threw me off-kilter because they came from some deeper part of me. I would have to start from scratch in my career as a massage therapist. I'd spent three decades building a clientele in Los Angeles, and now I would erase it all with one swipe. My former life didn't matter. What mattered was my granddaughter. That first night, I envisioned Erika as a child desperate and in danger of emotionally drowning and being forced to move along a river. I saw her near death from the rapid current. I had been so desperate and scared about saving her. But now Egan was helping me.

To be honest, I *was* nervous about raising a child again, especially one emotionally harmed by a murder. But there was no turning back. Egan handed me a tissue.

"Erika is the chance I have to take," I declared solemnly.

In my mind, I foresaw the difficulties ahead, even if I won custody. Would Erika and I be close, or would she have an unconscious resentment of me for switching places with her mother? Charla had been a breathtaking, charming beauty. I was a wrinkled old woman.

As Egan answered a question that Christopher asked, I closed my eyes and said a prayer for Erika and me. This little girl and I would be journeying together along a rocky trail. No doubt I would stumble, but I was betting on love—that love would eventually get us through.

"Soorya, if you are solidly on board, then so am I. I will do my absolute best to make everything succeed so you can get legal custody of your granddaughter. I'll also look out for Erika regarding her inheritance."

Too tired to talk, I simply said, "I'm grateful," reached over and squeezed Egan's hand.

Christopher shook Egan's hand next and said, "I was afraid for my mother having to do all of this on her own in Reno, but now with you, I know she'll be okay."

"I'm glad I'm available for this. The process will be difficult, but we will do it together as a team."

Egan Walker never once mentioned money until the end. He quoted us half the hourly rate that all his other peers quoted.

We sealed our commitment, and I took a deep breath of relief.

Outside, under the vast Reno open sky with fluffy clouds, I realized how blessed I was. Even though evil had attacked my family, we would triumph.

Once Egan came on board, life got better. The fretful worrying about unknown factors disappeared. Egan had handed me a protective mitt for the freezing pole. Better yet, the pole disappeared. Being with him felt more like when I'd held stones at the river. That same sense of grounding returned.

Later, Christopher, Geni, and I called Shawn Meador and took turns thanking him profusely on speaker phone.

I found out soon after that Egan cancelled his summer vacation with his family, locked himself in his office after obtaining all the files from Charla and Darren's divorce proceedings, and pored over each affidavit and motion to catch up.

And then another spectacular occurrence arrived. An angel entered the picture.

"Hello. My name is Ann Mudd. Your daughter was a friend of mine. I want to help. My parents are leaving town in a couple of weeks. Would you guys be interested in staying at their house? It's cute and clean and on a quiet street."

I will never forget that day. Not only did we find our perfect lawyer, but we also would gain a temporary home, which meant we could leave the noisy motel, where strangers slammed car doors and straggled by at all hours of the night. Better yet—it would be more appropriate for having Erika with us.

Ann said she would meet us the next day with a key. It would still be a couple of days before her parents left but that was okay. After we hung up, my anxiety about moving and breaking down my former life still lingered. But now, the frightened, panicked kid inside me subsided. Between Egan and Ann, I found renewed courage.

That night Christopher said, "Mom, you also have to get your massage license for Reno. Have you looked into those requirements yet?"

"I'll put that on my list," I smirked at Geni and then wanted to throw up. The thought of studying anatomy and taking a test caused a new burning sensation to drip from my head. "Let me give you guys a chore—tomorrow we have to get our fingerprints re-done," I said, adding to the mental sludge pile.

We'd made a mistake the day before doing our fingerprints at the police station, and paid around $70 each, only to find out we had to do them over again through Social Services. "We can't use your recent prints," they said. "They go into another government system, and it's not transferable to the FBI—sorry."

Notwithstanding the cost, time, and stress of re-doing our fingerprints, it just seemed so silly that agencies can't transfer that sort of information back and forth to each other!

Chapter 8
Hard Not to Hate

I started taking short walks alone each day. It wasn't as inspiring as my predawn sun rituals in Los Angeles, mainly because I had more faith and inspiration then. Still, Reno's natural beauty helped expand me. While Christopher and Genicia slept, I walked to the store to buy some food. A newsstand displayed another headline about Darren in the *Reno Gazette-Journal.* A smaller article below caught my eye, "Friends Loved Charla Mack." Tears fell. It featured two women who I didn't know. Francine Beard said, "Charla Mack could light up a room. Everyone loved her. She would walk into a room, and the energy inside would shift. She was bright and vibrant, energetic, and giving."

The article stated Beard was the former director of Cambridge Montessori School, which had since closed. Beard said when she interviewed for the school position in 1997, Charla and Darren were members of the parent board. "She's one of the reasons why I came here," Beard said. "She was beautiful inside and out. She was the best mother. She put a lot of energy into being a mom. It's not an easy thing to be a step-parent. I saw a lot that others didn't see and saw how hard she worked to make her family situation work. I can't tell you how special her children are, and that didn't happen by accident."

Beard also said she had loved Darren and had been "blown out of the water over his behavior."

The other board member, Sylvia Crawford, said, "Charla was always vivacious and had a lot of energy. She was always smiling and was just a good person."

Both Beard and Crawford agreed. "Charla was known for her exquisite scrapbooks and photographs."

Crawford commented, "Charla could have been a lazy rich mom who dropped her kids off and not have participated at the school, but instead, she was always there, helping the staff and helping other children as well."

Soon, one of Charla's closest friends, Chandra Mayer, called.

"Soorya, I want to warn you about Charla's landlord, Anne Savage. She's difficult."

"I appreciate your warning, but I'm good with people. I'll appeal to her humanity. I'm sure I'll be fine."

There was no assurance in Chandra's response. "Just to give you a head's up, Lisa flew in from Los Angeles the same night Charla died. She and I rushed over to Charla's house and pulled her valuables out of the safe. I had a key and removed Charla's ring and watch. Anne showed up and said someone had already broken into the house. Somehow she could tell that even though she'd locked the house."

"Since Darren was suing Charla for her wedding ring and watch, do you think it was his family trying to grab her jewelry?"

"We can't prove that, but it's fishy that no one stole the stereos or TVs, etc. Nothing we know of is missing. But we'd already retrieved the jewelry."

"Look, just by Anne's behavior toward us, she didn't respond lovingly or like you'd expect someone to deal with people after they've just lost a friend."

"Okay. Got it. I appreciate your call. I'll contact you as soon as I get into the house and let you know how it went."

Afterward, I thought about what to say to the landlord then dialed her number. "Hello, is this Anne?"

"Yes, who is this?"

"I'm Charla's mother, Soorya. I wonder if my family and I could stay at Charla's for a couple of days, so we don't have to spend so much money on hotels? More than that, I'd also love to be in my daughter's space with my mom and aunt. It would be great for all of us to mourn in Charla's space—is that possible?"

"I can't do that because legally, I am responsible for all of Charla's possessions. You'll have to file a request, which I think is a court order stating who you are, and get it signed by a judge before I can even let you in."

"But I have to get clothes to bury my daughter and some of Erika's things …" My voice must have sounded desperate.

She repeated herself in a monotone. "You'll need to get the formal papers from your lawyer before you come over."

Anne continued, "I'm filming all of Charla's things. If anyone claims anything is missing, I can cover myself. I don't want legal complications coming down on me. If you want to get in for a few minutes to gather some of Erika's things, I'll concede to that, but you have to be in and out."

"Okay. Could I come in about an hour?"

"That's fine."

My family and I could mourn better and in a more healing way if we were around all of Charla's environment and belongings. Now Anne was tearing *even that* away. I could not understand this kind of detachment from another human being. I would have not only allowed those of a deceased loved one in, but I would also have brought over a few meals.

My expectation of our family uniting at Charla's was demolished within seconds; yet another devastation. *How could my heart hurt anymore?* I had envisioned being in my daughter's house amongst her things and sharing with my mom, aunt and cousins as we mourned our Charla. How could fate have brought me such an insensitive person who had no comprehension? Her fear of a legal attack was more significant than her compassion for those who lost their beloved. I had landed in another jagged part of hell.

I took a cab to my daughter's rental. She had barely settled herself. That house represented a new break for Charla, as she was finally done with a vicious, years-long divorce and custody fight with Darren, who had moved out of the home they had built together, or rather Charla had lovingly decorated. She had turned the entire attic into a playroom for the children with every kind of educational game she found. There was also a section of doll clothes and doll houses where Erika's friends loved to come and play with her.

Charla's rental was at the end of a cul-de-sac, facing the desert mountains, with no sound of traffic. The high desert has a stark beauty and I imagined what it would be like to sit out at night in the backyard. Charla would have loved that. Her favorite outing was to star gaze during the dark of the moon. She always kept a bag of marshmallows stuffed in the cupboard and found excuses to build campfires and melt s'mores.

Anne opened on the first knock. A tall woman, European looking. "Hello, nice to meet you. As I said on the phone, be quick. I have to get back to work."

"Got it. Where's Erika's room?"

"To the left. I'm going to do some weeding."

Right away, I found knitting tools, yarn, and a few games. After gathering a pile of children's clothing, I stuffed it into a suitcase sitting on the closet shelf. As I wandered around, I realized Charla hadn't decorated Erika's room since they had just moved in. Most of her stuff was still in boxes. Ironically, both Charla and I had moved around the same time. Erika didn't even have a bedspread yet. Charla had wanted to find her perfect choice—another wave of bitterness hit me.

Noises filtered through. Someone was in the house making conversation. I went to see who was in the living room.

Joan Mack marched in pushing her cousin Judy in a wheelchair. *What???* "Joan, why are you here?"

"Charla took a lot of things from the Palace and I want to get them back."

Joan didn't look in my direction as she was too busy sucking in every part of Charla's surroundings like a human vacuum cleaner. She hurried over and kneeled by the television set to see if any of her electrical equipment was there. Judy fixed a glare on me. She reminded me of a dog that bit me on the face when I was a kid. Her mouth tightly pinched, I got the impression she could have placed a curse on me if she'd had the power. She held the purest hatred anyone had ever thrown at me. As I defended myself by turning around so I couldn't see her, Joan trotted past, leaving Judy to sit and stare while she went into Charla's office. I'd never seen Joan move so fast or so fixated on anything. With me, she had always been at least an hour late for doing anything. After rummaging through Charla's boxes, she hurried to her bedroom. I wondered if Anne had given her a time limit as well.

Just then, Anne opened the front door. As soon as she came closer to me I asked in a quiet voice, "Why is Joan here at the same time as me?"

"Oh, I figured this way you are both equal and I stay inside the guidelines of what is legal. Are you finished yet?"

I was so shaken by Anne's response, I barely heard myself saying words. I think I mumbled, "I've had enough for now." What I wanted to say, is I've had enough of you wretched women.

Joan approached me in the hallway. I saw nothing in her arms. I wondered what Charla had from her store that was so precious. This pathetic scene made me shudder as I remembered the movie *Zorba The Greek* I'd watched in my youth. After the death of a villager, townspeople broke in and, as if picking meat off a bone, they removed every single material possession within seconds. The only thing left were the walls and floors.

Anne walked to the door holding some keys. "Have a nice rest of your day."

She shut the door as I stood on the porch with Joan and Judy still inside.

Just then Elise, Darren's sixteen-year-old daughter, called. She wept openly. "I drove from my house in Nevada City to be around Charla's things two days ago. The police were there going through the house, and they literally pulled me out of Charla's bed while I sobbed on her pillow, begging to stay. I desperately yearned to lay on her bed. But they refused to allow me that one grace. It was horrible."

"Elise, the same thing is happening to me now. I totally get it. Charla used to swear you two were soul mates."

"I know. I had just asked her if I could stay with her for part of the summer, and she said yes. We were so looking forward to it."

I rubbed my temples until they hurt, forcing myself to remember what goes on during wars, and realized that as bad as Elise's and my situation was, others have had it worse as soldiers or militia might have stormed through and demolished everything. They could have carted us off in trains to a camp somewhere to be murdered. Still, when abuse happens to you, everything is subjective and it's hard not to hate …

As I reached the sidewalk, I remembered that I'd taken a taxi. I mentally estimated I could hike a couple miles to Virginia Street and catch the bus. *The walk will be good for me.* Then I looked down at the heavy suitcase with Erika's things, changed my mind and called Christopher. "We'll be there in ten minutes."

"I'll walk down to the first part of the street just to get away from here. I'll wait for you on the street corner. Joan's here and you might run into her."

"Joan! Wow, Mom, I'm soooo sorry. That must have been stressful seeing her at Charla's house."

"Yup. See you soon."

As I sat on the curb, Chandra called. "Soorya, I completely forgot to tell you earlier that yesterday Detective Chalmers gave me some vital news. It will hit the press eventually."

"What is it?"

"A man named Dan Osborn called the police directly after being at Darren's condo when the crime took place. Darren's actions were his own in the incident, and Dan didn't know what would occur in his presence.

"Dan is a former high school friend of Darren's and had been staying with him for a couple of weeks until his place was ready for a move. Darren had called him on Sunday, the night before he killed Charla, and asked him if he would come back to take Erika to his mother's house for him because he said he had some 'stuff' to do. But things got mixed up."

"Things got mixed up?"

"Darren told him to arrive promptly at 9:00 am to pick up Erika. He said Charla suddenly jumped out of her car to shake his hand and introduce herself. Then Erika announced she was hungry, so Dan left Charla and Darren outside and took Erika into the house to get her some food.

"As soon as Dan closed the door, Erika told Dan she heard a dog barking fiercely. Dan said that, after he listened, he heard barking too and walked back to open the inside door of the garage to check what was occurring. But as he reached for the door handle, Darren burst through and ran past him. Darren said nothing, but had a bloody white towel wrapped around his arm.

"Dan's dog followed through after Darren, panting, acting nervous. The dog had blood sprayed all over his fur. At first, Dan thought his dog was injured. But after examining him, he realized it wasn't his dog's blood.

"That's when Dan became frightened for his and Erika's life. He knew it had to be Charla's blood. He maneuvered Erika out of the condo while Darren was still in the bathroom. When Dan got Erika and his dog into his car, he went around the corner to get out of sight of Darren's condo to call 911. Then he also drove to the wetlands and washed his dog. Dan said he didn't know what to do. He called the police twice, and the second time, Darren interrupted the call on another line. Dan came back online with the police and said that Darren had been so casual, it terrified him. Darren said, 'Hey man, what was your hurry to get out of my place?'"

Chandra continued. "Dan said Darren wanted him to bring Erika and meet him at Starbucks before taking her to his mother's. Though Dan suspected the worst, he accepted out of fear. He said all three of them sat together at Starbucks while Erika ate a lemon bar and Darren drank iced tea. How weird it was that Dan said Darren laughed and joked during the visit like nothing happened."

"Dan drove Erika to Joan's house afterward. He told Joan, 'I am afraid Charla has been seriously hurt.' Joan said, 'Now you are scaring me.' As soon as Dan left Joan's house, he went down to the police station and wrote out a report."

"Poor Dan. Darren betrayed him as well!"

"Right? That's what I thought. But now the police have even more evidence on Darren."

"Thanks for sharing this with me. I appreciate being in the loop. The detectives only had so much time to talk with me, and they didn't reveal any of this. Boy, I also have to say you were one hundred percent correct about Anne Savage. I didn't see that coming. As my mother would say, she's one for the books!"

"I'm so sorry to have been right. I wish I hadn't been."

"I've even talked my way out of speeding tickets, but Anne was impossible."

After Chandra and I hung up, Christopher and Genicia finally came. She spoke first. "Soorya, you okay?"

"I haven't gone crazy yet."

"Hi, Mom. How was the experience with Anne Savage?"

"Boy, have I got some stories for you guys."

My brain felt like someone had pushed it through a colander, and then baked pieces of it that burned.

Chapter 9
The Savages

June 16, 2006

Friday morning, we were still in our motel room. a patch of sunlight poured through the curtain and touched my face. No matter what, I still appreciated sunlight.

Christopher got out of bed first. Even though this space wasn't home, I felt relieved we were all together and safe in the same room. What I also understood from a higher level was that I would never take my son or daughter-in-law for granted again in this lifetime.

"Good morning, Mom," Chris said, scratching his head. "I'll take the first shower, then leave the bathroom for you girls."

"Morning, Geni. Did you sleep okay?"

"I woke up at 2 am. We are officially jet-lagged. Ugh."

"Oh, I forgot about the time change from India. I slept okay but tossed and turned and gritted my teeth about Anne for a long time."

As we talked, Egan phoned at 7:00 am. "Soorya, good morning. I got the proper papers from the judge by midnight.

Your family now has access to Charla's house—it's all clear! If you want to pick up the court order, I'll be in my office by 8:30. I'll leave the papers out in the front corridor on a table in case I'm with a client so you can access them."

"Egan! How incredible! We thought we'd have to wait until Monday for certain. Thank you so much, and we'll be there at 9:00."

Geni yelled into the bathroom, "Chris, it's all set. Egan got the papers!" When Christopher came out, we three slapped high fives. We drove to Egan's. As promised, the papers were in the front waiting room inside a pottery bowl folded neatly. I smiled.

Once we got back in the car, I called Anne Savage. "It's Soorya. I got the necessary papers this morning. May I come over sometime today and get what I need?"

"Really? Interesting." Anne's voice drifted off. I assumed she was thinking out loud. "Okay then. I'm surprised that procedure went so quickly. How about 1pm?"

"Great, see you then."

"You guys, I need some time by myself inside Charla's house first. Is that possible without hurting your feelings?"

"I think that's best, Mom," Christopher said. "And that gives us time to run over to check on my dad again. He's not doing too well."

"It sucks your dad lost Andrea too. I feel so bad for him."

"I know. I still can't believe she died on the same day as Charla. Andrea was eventually Robert's life partner after me. Andrea and I got along well, and I was grateful to have her on board because when Christopher stayed there she taught him etiquettes that I missed like refined table manners. When Chris graduated from Princeton University, she flew there to watch him accept his diploma and sat with me. We wept together, being proud of him the moment he accepted his diploma. I added, "Not only did she die on the same day, but on the same *morning*. It's cosmically uncanny--like they left together."

The thought of my former husband's partner dying of ovarian cancer the same morning my daughter was brutally murdered disassembled my rational mind.

"I'm sorry, Christopher, that you are going through two deaths at the same time."

"I know. My mind is whirling in shock like yours."

"All I know is I'm aching to be in Charla's house so I can feel her energy." I felt almost sick with anticipation.

On the ride over, I took another study of Charla's former neighborhood. It was quiet and the homes all had garages and looked built by the same contractor. Charla had said, "I rented this here because I want to make the large backyard a playground for Erika and her friends."

Anne greeted me at the door with her preteen son. Another woman, around thirty, rushed in from behind, stretched out her hand, "Hi, I'm Anne's daughter."

"And my daughter's a lawyer." Anne held her head up a little too high as I could see underneath her chin.

I nodded. *Oh great. Anne's daughter is probably the one who created all this fear and why Anne wouldn't allow me into the house to stay with my family even though Charla paid rent for at least two more weeks–and she had her deposits!*

"Well, hello." My hand went limp shaking Anne's.

I can't remember her daughter's name. I didn't want to remember her name. I knew she had come in case Anne needed an eyewitness if anything went "wrong."

"May I go to Charla's bedroom?" I asked nervously. "I need to get some clothes for her funeral."

"This way ..." Anne pointed as she led me down the hallway. Her daughter followed. Aside from grabbing Erika's clothes, I hadn't been in that house since she'd just moved in.

Once inside, grief overcame me. Her personality was everywhere. My emotions regressed into that frozen sensation again as I held onto the mahogany wood four-poster bed. Charla had placed a canopy of white linen over a rose-colored bedspread. She didn't have any pictures up yet, but her trusty treadmill was next to one wall. The story of the treadmill was both infuriating and hilarious. After Darren had left for good, he broke into the house when she was visiting a friend. As he came through the gate, he threw away the pins that made it work so there was no way for her to close it again to feel protected. He then drove a truck and rammed into the garage door, smashing it so she couldn't lift it any longer. Strangely, he also smashed a window to enter. He destroyed the snow blower so she couldn't clean her driveway. Once in, he stole her most precious things, including her treadmill. But he was so lazy and stupid that he placed everything into a storage unit that was still in Charla's name since their divorce wasn't final. He haphazardly threw everything into one spot including her Vera Wang wedding dress, exposed to be ruined, hanging on top of a pile of other things. Charla had felt victorious though, because she got it all back by simply getting an employee to open the unit.

She said, "I knew right away he would steal my photo albums to hurt me. I taped one to the inside of the fireplace with strong tape and the other inside the dog house. Darren would never lower himself to look in those two spots, especially the dog house!" She cackled. "But the way he destroyed the garage door made me truly afraid of him. I knew by how violent he smashed it; he was going for blood. We were selling that house but he didn't give a damn. I was grateful for Lisa flying in from LA that day to help me."

Just then, Anne's young son burst in. He loudly zoomed around, making sounds of racing cars. He turned and ran through the house, slamming the front door, then within seconds, back in and slammed the front door again.

Anne rushed over to one window. "I need to fix this," she muttered under her breath as she fidgeted with the casing and scraped something with her finger on the hinge.

I slid my legs down and sat on the plush carpet next to the nightstand, and picked up a box of Charla's CDs sitting under the bed.

I made every effort to ignore Anne while sorting through the music to find something appropriate for her funeral. I ached, yearning to be alone.

After safeguarding the lock, Anne said, "Excuse me," as she brushed past to enter the closet.

Her daughter, who had been standing at the door watching me, said, "Oh! I need some water," and left.

My breathing labored. Just to distract myself, I put a CD down on the carpet and pressed my head to my knees. As each second gathered, I grew more upset by their disturbances. I didn't want these women in my daughter's bedroom; I didn't want them around me as I chose a song for her funeral. *How can I think?*

"I'm back!" Anne's daughter smiled to herself as she joined her mother in the closet.

Their voices grew sharper; my mind sprouted a more core anger. I imagined finding a baseball bat and banging it on the wall, yelling, "Get out of here—how dare you!"

Anne burst back through the bedroom with an armload of blouses on her arm. "Soorya, I forgot to ask—how is the legal process coming along in relation to Darren?" She took a breath. "What's happening on the legal front concerning Erika—anything new to report from Social Services? How do you like your new lawyer? Is everything in the news reports true about Darren? What's it like seeing him on television?"

As Anne kept pommeling me with questions, it was all I could do not to shove the old banana I had in my purse into her mouth. I had fallen into a torture chamber.

Infuriated, I mumbled, "Not sure about any of that."

Anne nodded and moved back into the closet. The rattle of hangers clanged as if hitting something. I got up and sat on the bed so I could get a better view of what they were doing. I had to watch them. They continued to pick through Charla's clothes like at a primo garage sale. Anne pulled out Jackets and more blouses; her daughter, on the opposite side, dresses.

Anne rushed past me to throw clothes onto Charla's bed. Her daughter followed with bulging armloads.

The angrier I got, the quieter I became, but inside I was aching to bang pans and scream, "Go away and leave me alone!"

I wanted to shout to the entire city what freaks they were.

Both women now stood so close to me, that I felt Anne's arm hairs brush against my arm until she moved slightly back. She sounded pleased. "Here's something for *you,* Soorya! I think this would fit you, and it's very stylish."

Her daughter chimed, "Here, try this for the funeral." She held out a blue chiffon dress—with a grin so wide her teeth stood out like a donkey's.

"Now, *this* is something Charla could wear in her casket!" Anne's voice blew like a swirling high pitch tone.

"Wait—or what about this one? Maybe this orange paisley dress?" her daughter asked.

It felt like they were killing my daughter all over again. I kept hoping they might catch an emotional clue.

"Okay, this is the *one*. It's a perfect choice—the peach-colored suit would be just right for her skin tones!" Anne chimed.

My voice wavered as I reached for a tissue on the nightstand. "She needs something to cover the stab wound on her neck ..."

Anne's forehead wrinkled, and she tilted her head to the side as if studying my words. I suspected she'd never thought of Charla's injuries.

"Rightie then. We can find a turtleneck top to go with this suit because you must, must use this suit. It's the best!" The two nodded their heads in agreement.

Their energy was like coffee beans brewed on beds of steroids. I said nothing, but I could barely contain myself.

"I'm going in again," Anne said, depicting a hero fireman.

They both clicked their heels at the same time. I was so spent I moved the piles of clothes to lay down on a spot next to the pillow. I thought about how renting someone else's space could be not only tenuous, but an absolute nightmare.

Both marched back with yet another heap of clothing. "Oh, what's the matter—you tired?" Anne asked, titling again as she landed the clothes to the side of my leg.

"Most likely."

"Maybe rest for a while."

"That's my plan," My tone was now as chilling as possible.

Standing there studying me, possibly like one would a mannequin in a store setting, Anne grabbed another top. "If you don't use the suit, this is my second choice."

Every muscle in my body felt like someone was tackling and hogtying me for a competition. Determined not to show seething-ness, I remained still. Because being in my daughter's last living space was so overwhelmingly nourishing for my soul, and I didn't want to sully any possibility that would get me thrown out.

I wondered if they felt guilty for not allowing me and my family to stay. Was this their way of making it up to me? God, how I wished I had asked Christopher to come with me!

Anne dropped the same suit on my lap. She clearly wanted me to use it. "That won't fit her. Could I please make these choices by myself? I need to be alone to look through her things. But thank you for your help."

"Okay," Anne nodded her head. "But I *did* see one more terrific blouse in there."

Her daughter came out and tapped on the closet door to get attention. "Hey—I'm going back to work."

Anne's son joined in for the fifth time. "Mom, something's going on outside!" He ran out just as fast.

"I need to check on what he's talking about. We are leaving now, so call us as soon as you finish and I'll drive back to lock up."

I held my breath then spoke. "Sure."

Once they were all gone, I staggered into the bathroom and patted cold water on my face. Since Charla's death, I had splashed more water on my face than at any time in my life.

It was a weeknight, and what made everything worse was that Anne had pressured me to be out early because of her work schedule. It was impossible to shake off my grief that I couldn't spend the night there.

I came out of the bathroom to hear a meow. It was my cat, Tara! I remembered how Anne admitted to the detectives that she had accidentally locked her in the closet with no food or water for several days. Like Sparkles locked in Darren's garage, Tara had suffered, too. As I petted my cat, I felt further fury, resenting all humans who lacked sensitivity and hurt animals. *I'm grabbing Tara as soon as I get settled!*

But the nightmare wasn't over: Anne suddenly barged back in. "Oh, I forgot something." Her tone, the most serious so far.

With eyebrows furrowed, this woman extended her hand dangling a plastic bag. "What do you want to do about *this*?" She held the bag close.

It was Charla's masturbation paraphernalia.

Part of me wanted to tell her exactly where to put it. I considered saying, "Take it as a gift from me to you."

Instead, "Can you get rid of it? I don't want it in the trash in case the media goes through it."

"Oh, right." she looked perplexed as if a moral decision must be made, then walked away.

She had exterminated every drop of finesse inside of me. I had never been so embarrassed. It wouldn't matter what I said to Anne. Anyone who would not allow a family to grieve together was already so out of touch with their humanity, she couldn't possibly understand what she had just presented to me might be mortifying.

Once Anne departed for the second time, carrying Charla's precious personal, I gave myself a pep talk: *Pull yourself together. Take in the essence of your daughter's energy. Remember, this is it.*

Charla's treadmill at the side of her bed. A draped bathrobe over a chair.

Memories everywhere: her toothbrush and face cream, her brush with lingering hair. Cha Cha had a lion's mane and couldn't shampoo more than once a week, or her curls became frizzy.

No further mayhem would ruin my precious time. I sat on the floor again, sorting the CDs as quickly as possible. While listening to some song, the ceiling light directly above me flickered and turned off. *Hmmm, another distraction...* Now, it was harder to read the print on the cases. I sighed. *Lousy luck. I can't seem to catch a break.* The light bulb must have burned out.

I moved to another wall near the treadmill. As I played the next song, that ceiling light went dark as well. *What?* The system had to be faulty even though it was a relatively new house. *Darn! I'll never get the music together in such a short time frame.*

After a while, the floor felt hard. To take a short break, I laid my head down on Charla's bed again to the one open spot not overloaded with clothes. Her water bed swooshed underneath, comforting me.

Just as I drifted to sleep, the light directly above that had been off, turned on. It beamed so brightly, chills secreted through me. I knew. Without a doubt, I knew it was Charla attempting to contact me.

Not only did the light stay on, but now all the bulbs in the ceiling went off and on around the room, almost like they were playing a concert with each other. Two lights would come on, then go off, and then another two would beam on. This light show was feisty, like my daughter. It reminded me of the scene from the movie Ghost. "Move a penny, Charla." I said out loud. I needed to laugh after so much chaos with Anne and her daughter.

Charla had the same exuberant energy on the other side as she had on Earth. I once read about people taking in data recorded that loved ones recently crossing over to the side consistently use communicating through the flashing/electrical technique. Here I was experiencing it first-hand. On and off it went for another ten minutes. If only her spirit that had shown itself through the colors of green and blue could come now and embrace me!

I imagined this was an accomplishment for an out-of-body person. "Wow, honey, you've only been on the other side for less than a week. I'm impressed with how well you're doing!"

Once the light show stopped, and almost like the way the ribbon of a measuring tape fiercely snaps back into its case, a downtrodden despair covered my heart, much like a stale and overly milky, turning rotten dessert.

Tara trotted in purring, seeking attention. Time to shift. Time to let go. The last hour had been glorious. Within ten minutes I picked a song and an outfit. Peach blouse she wore a lot. I used pajama bottoms since viewers at the funeral home wouldn't see them and they would be easy for the mortician to slip on. Plus, Charla almost lived in pajamas at home.

I was cleaning up the piled clothes mess when Christopher and Geni yelled to me from the entrance.

I darted to the front door. "I'm happy to see you guys!"

Christopher held a bag of groceries. "Good, Mom. I hope you had some time for yourself. We didn't buy any condiments because we knew Charla had them."

Too spent from the earlier ordeal, I didn't mention anything yet. "Nice, you brought food. Charla has a toaster oven too."

Genicia turned on the light in the kitchen while Christopher unloaded the food on the counter. I opened the refrigerator door to grab a couple of condiments. A bolt of lightning hit me and I let out a high-pitched sound. Everything was gone — not one condiment, nothing. The only thing left in Charla's refrigerator, which was formerly stuffed, was a case of cheap beer.

I gasped for air as I saw that every. Single. Thing: GONE. I had lived with Charla and knew her fridge always bulged with food. Anne now enraged me on a new level. This time, it was a tornado emerging from my head. All of my daughter's high-quality items were missing, like flaxseed and avocado oils, mayonnaise from the health food store, assortments of mustards, ketchup made with date sugar for Erika, specialty vinegars, soy sauce, etc. I opened the freezer, and that was empty, too. Charla's frozen pizzas and other entrees she'd cooked for Erika, gone. I had envisioned eating those ice creams and popsicles. I quickly called Anne.

"Anne, I just opened Charla's fridge, and all the food is missing—what happened?"

"Oh ... I thought the court order would take a lot longer. I thought everything would rot, so I threw it out to save time."

"You had no right to do that. We could have used those condiments for months, and all the frozen food would have helped our budget! Frozen foods don't rot."

"Well, what's done is done." Her excuse infuriated me more. "I'll be over in a little while. I have to go." She hung up on me. She fucking hung up on me.

I suspected she took the condiments for herself. Here it was again. Anne Savage had stolen more of my daughter's energy from me. In earlier years, a landlord had violated me by slipping into my rental when I was out of town. She'd cleaned everything in my house to get it "ready" for the next tenant since I was moving—washed all my delicate things, even an expensive silk blouse that still had a price tag on it. She shrunk it because she'd placed it in scalding water and into a hot dryer with the towels. This horrid woman had also trashed all my son's precious artwork. I experienced the same violation and rape of rights now as I felt then. It took me years to overcome my upset with that experience and the trigger for it was here again. I walked over, sat in a chair, and placed my head on the dining table. It was too much. Another savage had ravaged me.

Ten minutes later, Anne opened the door with her husband, Rick. Her first words: "Are you guys almost done? I need to lock up."

"How *dare* you violate us like this!"

Anne's body shook so hard I thought she might piss her pants. Her eyebrows touched, her lower lip protruded in a pout, like she might slobber on herself. She grabbed her cell and punched numbers, shrieking, "I'm calling the police!"

Rick protested. "Let's all calm down. I'm sure we can work this out."

My thought was "Only if you replace everything in the fridge ..."

Anne kept pushing numbers and missing. Her hands shook too much. After the fifth failure, she braced herself against the wall, panting like a bulldog, leaving her texting arm to dangle.

I raised my voice. "How *could* you have possibly taken all my daughter's food out of her fridge without talking to me first?"

Anne's eyes now blackened. "I swear I'm calling them! You have no right!" She grabbed her phone again as if to intimidate me, but she was so nervous she still couldn't punch a simple 911 through.

Rick reached over and put his hand on her arm. "Why don't you give it a break. Let's talk this through."

The way her body and hands shook was noteworthy and a study for insane asylums. She jerked away from him and placed her phone on the kitchen counter. I was seething. I didn't need to talk anything over. I was a dragon blowing fire in her direction. Rick looked at me and said, "Anne's right, what's done is done."

I wanted her to write me a check for $400.00 for the stolen goods. I completely forgot about Charla's deposits. She was getting off cheap. Christopher shook his head and curled his lips while commanding. "Yes, what she did is what she did, and I can't stand being in this house for another second. Let's go, Mom."

Chris gathered our bag from the counter. Anne was now leaning over the sink still shaking. Rick walked with us to open the front door. He said under his breath, "I'm so sorry you had to go through all that."

"I can see you are at least a real human being, and I'm grateful for your compassion. Thank you."

Rick offered his hand to Chris, and he took it. Geni and Rick exchanged a few words. I wanted to add, "You *do* realize how nuts your wife is though—right?" But I stuffed my bristled dragon's tail under me and said nothing.

As we drove away, Geni said, "Boy, I never want to see that woman again."

"I agree. It will be a searing hot day in Antarctica before I forget this experience. I never fathomed that this kind of human existed, let alone would pop up after losing Cha Cha. I assumed her landlord would be compassionate and loving."

"Mom, do you want to have that icy orange juice you like?"

"Sounds perfect."

Who knew that the pleasure of Jamba Juice would be what kept me off meds after dealing with such a savage.

Chapter 10
The Viewing

In the depths of unspeakable grief, in the whirlwind of preparations for a custody battle with one of the wealthiest families in the state of Nevada, we had a funeral to plan. We chose Mountain Mortuary, in northwestern Reno, off of I-80 because of its beautiful location facing the Sierra Nevada mountains, which Charla loved.

Kim Garret joined Christopher, Genicia and I at the mortuary. As we opened its large wooden doors, we saw a cheerful, large room brightly lit by tall windows. The centerpiece of the room was a wooden table with brochures. If not for the advertisements for funeral arrangements, we could have been in a realtor's office. A man with glasses in a loose gray suit entered.

"You came to see Mrs. Mack?"

"Yes."

"That is fine, but I think you should look at our stock of coffins first." Christopher sighed. "Oh, that's right." He shrugged his shoulders. "We need a casket."

Kim stayed behind as the man led the three of us into an annexed room with full rows of coffins, many elaborate.

"Christopher, I believe in cremation for ecological reasons, but I'm having second thoughts since the children are still so young."

"Mom, I agree. They might want to visit her—to see her grave."

A casket it was.

We settled on the least expensive one. No surprise there. We knew it would be impractical to waste cash for something dissolved in the dirt.

Next, we chose the grave marker. We made sure she was identified as Charla Marie Sampsel, her maiden name, with no trace of the venomous Mack family.

Entering the next room, Christopher howled in inconsolable, screeching tones. Geni placed her arms around him to help steady his trembling. I wanted to shift gears, hug and rock him in my arms, but my instincts held back, feeling he needed to go through the process—better medicine to get it out.

Christopher's crying lapsed into body tremors as he laid his head on Geni's shoulder.

"Mom, I can't take it. Can't do this … can't see Charla. I have to sit this one out." Geni and I nodded.

"No problem, son,"

Geni looked at Christopher. "I'll go with your mom."

Kim came to support us in silence still, as she had been quiet all this time. She moved to the chair near Chris. almost like a female Buddha.

Genicia firmly placed her arm through mine, and we followed the funeral director to another area. Her touch felt strong and sturdy, like she was entirely present and up to the challenge of whatever the experience was. The mortician waited for us in an empty room. He sat on a stool and looked up with raised eyebrows. "Miss Townley, she isn't … isn't made up yet. What I mean is it's … it's going to be too gruesome for you to look at her."

He pulled out a hankie from his pocket to wipe his forehead. "Most people don't want to see their beloveds until they're made up."

Maybe he thinks I'm going to freak out, and he'll have a screaming mess on his hands.

I glared back. "I want, no, *need to* know what my daughter went through. I need to see her body untouched."

His eyes softened. "Oh okay, and it's your right." He guided us through a short hall to another room. A body with a sheet over it laid on the table. As Geni and I held onto each other tightly, the man gently lowered the sheet down to Charla's stomach.

It's challenging to explain what I experienced seeing her.

I remembered Charla when she'd had her first ballet lesson; the time she impulsively kissed a boy her age on the cheek at age three. I took a picture of her as it was so endearing. Now here she was in a decomposed state of the flesh.

I don't know if I'll ever be able to define how hollow I felt. If you travel at the speed of light, it takes eight minutes to get to the sun, one minute to arrive on the moon. But the emptiness of a ravaged heart takes billions of years to mend. At least mine does.

Charla's stab wounds were more severe than the detectives reported. The main cut went through each muscle and tendon in her neck and penetrated her carotid artery. The entire neck was open to the bone. Atrophy had set in and forced the tissue to widen even more extensively. I lifted the lower sheet. There were wounds all over her legs. Her broken, jagged fingernails told the story of fighting desperately to live.

"Mommy's here, darling, my sweet baby. I will love you forever." I held on to Geni's arm. Her mental strength, although she cried quietly, was that of a soldier on duty.

I leaned down and whispered, "I'm so sorry." I knew Charla was long gone, and there was no way to find her spirit in the decay. Geni whimpered. I moved closer to my daughter and stroked her beautiful wavy brown hair. She had been to the hairdresser recently, and had applied blond streaks layered around her face. I touched her cheek. Just as my finger brushed her eyebrow, the mortician shook his head, reached out, and grabbed my hand to make me stop. For his sake, I pulled back.

"It's too much," he said.

I didn't understand what was too much. It wasn't like I was slobbering kisses on her. *Why is everyone curtailing me from grieving one way or another?* He'd already announced that he thought it improper that I was there at all. I sighed, then took one for the team. "Thank you for letting me see her." My voice fell further away.

"You're welcome, Ms. Townley, and truly, I hope viewing her brought you the closure you needed."

I had studied a cadaver at a medical school during professional training in Los Angeles and was grateful that the experience prepared me for viewing Charla. Still, the jolt of how staggeringly deep her wounds were would stay with me for life.

I hugged Genicia. "For you to be with me and to do what you just did—I want you to know I will never forget how brave and strong you were today. You are my hero now. Our relationship has elevated to a new level. I will never forget how you supported me."

"I'm grateful to be here for you, Soorya hermosa. It would have been too much for you to be alone."

"How are you such a strong person at such a young age?"

"When I lived in Nicaragua, there was a civil war. As a child, I had to walk the streets and step over dead bodies. It happened more than once, and it made me strong."

"My God, it's unfathomable how much humans suffer, especially children."

"Children go through hell, especially during war."

Geni and I held each other and rocked our bodies in the darkened hall. After a while, we met up with Christopher and Kim. My son sat on a chair. His eyes stared off into space. "Mom, thank you for not pushing me."

"Oh, honey, we all have our limits."

Christopher's face was gray and, under his eyes, puffy. He kept yanking at patches of his hair.

Later we drove to a restaurant and purchased a paper from a newsstand. The *Reno Gazette-Journal* reported the police had released the video from the parking structure where Darren had shot Judge Weller.

An FBI profiler gave an interview about Darren:

"That's a hell of a shot. I mean that is an absolute hell of a shot, especially for someone knowing they already had committed a homicide. The shooter knew where the high ground was and knew there was a clear shot to [Weller's] office, and his emotions don't get in the way of accuracy. It's hard to believe he was able to put that together within two hours without some forethought or planning. So, he was practiced in the long shot and probably made long shots in the past. So, we have one killing that looks like an unplanned emotional outburst and another cold, calculated killing that suggests planning and forethought. My challenge would be to put these aspects together. When I look at this guy's background, I think he considers he is the sun, and everyone else is the planets that circle him. I think he's the most important person in his mind right now, and his children are probably secondary."

"Geni, Chris, look! There was also a letter to the editor about Charla in the personals."

Article was a low blow to Charla family, and friends

The Marie Claire article written by Amanda Robb is trash journalism at best. At worst, it's another breathtaking blow to Charla Mack's family and friends. She was also a daughter, a sister, and a mother. She was loyal, and she was kind and she was stabbed to death.

With freedom of speech comes great responsibility. Instead of showing compassion about the murder of a beautiful human being, Ms. Robb decided to throw another punch at those of us still standing in the ring with blackened eyes and bloody noses, fighting for the dignity of Charla who can no longer speak for herself.

Christine Libert, Reno

I felt admiration and gratefulness to Christine. At that exact moment my cell rang. "Soorya, this is Chandra. Do you want to meet somewhere right now? I have more information from the police."

"Good timing. We were just walking into the Thai place that Charla loved."

Chandra Meyer was Charla's best friend in Reno. When Chandra entered through the glass door, I remembered how stunning she was: silky blond hair, tiny stature, and wide hazel-green eyes. Perfect features. She resembled a fairy.

After we ordered food, Chandra said, "I have friends on the police force. Once Darren finished killing our Charla, he removed her cell from her car, and as he drove north towards Sacramento, he threw it out the window." Chandra continued. "An intuitive police officer had a feeling that Darren might do that. He kept walking along the freeway, and sure enough, he heard her phone ringing next to a bush and brought it back to the station. That was a major lead because they knew Darren had split from Reno."

I picked up my cloth napkin and wiped my eyes. "I'm sure her phone kept ringing from friends calling; I still call that number to hear her voice."

"Right? Me too," Chandra looked off into the distance. No words to be said. We had a blessed moment of silence before my phone rang.

"Soorya Townley?"

"Yes."

"This is Detective Ron Chalmers. I just wanted you to know we've tracked Darren to Mexico. We're closing in on him."

Chapter 11
The Circus of Death

"I'm beyond relieved. I was terrified that Darren might grab Erika."

"I want you to be in the loop, and I'll call you as soon as there's more information."

"How did you find Darren so fast?"

"Lead Detective John Ferguson is clever with technical stuff. He's been tracking Darren's email address, from different sites and where he lands. Plus, we had an eyewitness who recognized him in Mexico."

"That figures."

"I can't stay on long because I'm at work, but do you have any questions?"

"No, I'm thrilled that things are moving fast. Thanks for calling. You've made my month."

We all clapped and cheered. It relieved me that Chandra was with us for the news.

After we ate, my mother called to let me know she and Aunt Jackie were almost to Reno from Kingman, Arizona. We agreed they would stay next to us at the Atlantis Hotel. My cousins from California would come the next day.

It was 9:00 pm and I was tired but we walked down to greet my mother and aunt. I knocked on the door with apprehension—mainly because I felt terrible for her about Charla. She opened the door, hugged us, and attempted to move her lips to a smile. Aunt Jackie sat on the edge of the bed with a pained frown while rummaging through her purse. She muttered, "Lord have mercy." That was always the signal that she and my mother were upset.

Despite our hopeless predicament, it felt comforting to be together. My mom's lip kept quivering. "Christopher, even though I'll never get over losing our precious Charla, I'm happy to see you and Genicia, at least."

"I agree, Grandma." He reached out and gave her another hug.

My mom, who was approaching eighty, rubbed her eyes. She had the darkest rings under them I'd ever seen as if she had wept too many times. "Soorya, since Christopher just moved to India, I thought I might never spend time with him again."

"I know, Grandma. I'm happy to see you too. You're right—at least we have this." Christopher's drawn, puffy face looked like he'd been crying too.

"Was the open sky along that route beautiful?" I asked, shifting the subject. "Yes, spectacular." My Aunt Jackie's voice lifted.

"I was hoping you guys would have a beautiful drive, at least." Christopher kept his arm around my mom.

We shared stories about Erika and what had been going on with Charla's landlord. My mother said with her Kentucky drawl, "I'd like to get a hold of that Anne in a dark alley."

"Mom, you just made me laugh."

"Why don't you both settle in? I bet you're tired from all the driving."

"Boy, you can say that again," my mom said.

I remembered the night my mother met Darren. In parting, she had declared loudly, "You better not hurt my baby, or I'll kill ya."

My mother added under her breath, "If this monster doesn't get the death penalty, then one of us needs to get a gun and shoot him."

She meant it. The day my mom had threatened Darren, his face hadn't changed as he turned his back on her and joked with my brother John as if she hadn't spoken.

At dawn, my phone rang. "Hey, it's Lanny. Our family would like to meet you over at Social Services for something vitally important."

"What's this about?"

"I'd rather talk in person." I'd never heard him sound so serious. "Can you arrive, say, around 9:00 and meet us at Social Services?"

"Okay, I'll change appointments so I can be there." I hung up, annoyed we couldn't just talk over the phone.

⬧

Diane Wozinack greeted us as soon as we entered a small building off a busy street and I couldn't guess where we were. It looked like an annex to the library. The tall trees around the building provided shade. Inside, the room had a circular conference table designed for around twenty people. Lanny, Joan, and two men sat huddled, whispering to each other. One man stood up. "Hello, I'd like to introduce myself. I'm Paul. Joan and Lanny have contracted me to protect Erika."

The other man said his name so quietly I didn't catch it. I assumed Lanny had hired him as well. "Paul here is a retired sheriff," Lanny said, as he pressed his hand on top of Paul's shoulder. Then turned his head away as he took a deep breath. "This is a crazy time, and we're afraid someone might attempt to kidnap Erika because she's high profile right now. I want her safeguarded when she's with you. Our family believes she should stay in a hotel that has top security. We've hired these two men to watch over her and also to drive you to your hotel and from the funeral, and to the gravesite."

I wanted to say something sarcastic. *Hmm, so you've already hired these men without my family deciding. Then what decision do I have to make?*

I wasn't mocking Lanny, but it was just one more complication. I couldn't think past Charla being gone, getting her funeral arrangements in order, and dealing with a custody case—plus now my mother, aunt, and cousins had arrived. The thought of Erika potentially being kidnapped for ransom overloaded the imaginary cinder blocks on my back. I wanted to demand that they leave me alone, then stomp out. Why was I so timid?

Lanny continued, "The guards and I think you'll be safe at the Circus Circus Hotel because it's large, and we've already rented a car for you guys. This is the kind of thing that puts children in their greatest danger."

My bouncing knee under the table kept banging into a steel rod fixture. I thought Lanny's plan sounded more dangerous because thousands of humans walked around a highly populated casino area. *It would be easier for someone to hide ...*

Christopher had a glazed expression. Geni squeezed my hand under the table.

The room took a pause. Not even Diane threw out any other possibility. The nameless guy, around fifty with brown hair, slumped his body over with elbows on the table. He never looked up; I couldn't see his facial features. Reddish blond-haired Paul, around forty, kept clenching and unclenching his jaw.

Something I couldn't place felt fishy. "This is going to be a hassle, since my family is staying at the same hotel we're at, and I don't want to move. I want to be next to my mother," I stammered.

Lanny repeated his mantra, "Soorya, there are people out there who prey on small children, and you don't want to take any chances."

I ached to belt out, "Boy, are you right! And one of them is your psychopath brother who put her in the worst harm's way a week ago."

"Mom, it's your decision," Christopher startled me out of my confusion.

"All right, Lanny. I'll move to the new hotel as long as you guys pay for Lisa and her daughters coming in from LA to stay annexed to our room."

"Oh, right—Lisa was Charla's best friend."

"I also want Erika with us the entire time, to be with her friends."

"Sure, we can agree to that," Lanny said.

Joan stared down, offering nothing. *I wonder how she feels about this … she is mysterious.* My breath declined as I sat immobile. I couldn't find a snail of courage to express my instincts that this scheme was overly dramatic.

At least we would have Erika with us the entire time Lisa and her daughters were there.

Everyone filed out, and I was the last to leave. Diane came back into the room and to my side. "Well, they seem bent on this, and at least you get a bigger room to stay in." She patted my arm.

I felt the same bamboozled feeling I had with Anne Savage, who refused my family to mourn at her house. I wanted to throw chairs against the wall. It was astounding how me and my family couldn't find a spoonful of serenity.

The next day after I packed up from Atlantis, the Mack team instructed the guards to drive Erika and I to Circus Circus Hotel, where Paul would register us under another name. Christopher and Geni would stay with his father in Sparks, next to Reno. I later found out that Paul had an 'in' with the hotel manager. He was getting us in for free.

In cases of homicide when the murderer is still at large, the State of Nevada provides shelter for the bereaved family for a brief time. I feared the state would cancel helping us after my excursion to a hotel out of their stipulation. I didn't have a job yet. What if something went wrong and Ann Mudd's parents came home early? My thoughts designed fear webs around me.

"Paul, how long are you comping us?"

"I can do two nights."

Ah, okay. So, then we'll be on our own, I guess. Because the State of Nevada might finish their financial help.

My thoughts were on fire, living moment to moment. All those life-affirmative sayings my friends and I had used over the years about letting go of attachments were now testing me. I knew the real grind of letting go, and having faith, was by far more challenging than merely reading about it in a book or taking a seminar. The simple fact was even though I was annoyed about leaving the Atlantis Hotel, I surrendered to Lanny's paranoia as I didn't want to be wrong about someone grabbing Erika. Plus, it relieved me to have my granddaughter be with her friends.

The two guards left me in the casino lobby, saying they'd meet us in the morning. Since Christopher and Geni had gone to be with his dad, I had that same empty feeling as when Marilyn left. The emotional train of emptiness rushed along its tracks again and pushed me inside a locked trolley car. Back in it again.

After sleeping pills providing solid sleep, the morning arrived. Our guard, Paul, called on the hotel phone and said both men were down in the lobby, ready to escort me to my new digs, the Circus Circus Hotel. I picked up my purse, suitcase and bag of toiletries and went to meet the guards in the lobby. As I walked toward the two men, I couldn't shake off my resentment not being able to remain near my mother and aunt. I remembered my first thought in the car at my apartment when my body couldn't turn on the air conditioning. I'd landed in a world out of my control.

Paul stood to the side in a bright blue shirt with an unlit cigarette between his fingers. I wondered why I couldn't ask the other guy his name. His demeanor seemed too distant, and he kept folding and unfolding his arms as he stood across the lobby from Paul. It was as if he didn't want to be with us, so I left him alone. Paul was his usual cool self—always a gentle expression, but never present to eye contact or intimacy.

My stomach dropped. "Where's Erika?"

"Lanny will bring her by in a while."

"Oh, okay," I said, disappointed that she wasn't with us already.

I listened to the guards talk as we drove. They used acronyms, and I thought it was code. Paul said, "If we get to the MT before lunch, be sure to TAT." He turned to me, "Soorya, we have to let you out in front of the casino because we have another assignment."

"Oh ... But I thought you were here to walk in with me and stick around to make sure Erika's safe?"

"Sorry, but you'll have to call us again because we have to go."

Bubbles, in my imagination, erupted from laughter. I was bursting to say, "Some guards you guys are."

The Circus Circus Casino complex was at the end of downtown Reno, off a freeway with no access to any supermarkets within walking distance. The cacophony of gambling, blazing lights, shrill sirens, and smoke overwhelmed me. As I walked further into the noise, my left leg cramped. I hobbled through rows of slot machines where women sat with cigarettes hanging off their mouths as their fingers placed coins continually in the slots. An old man chewing tobacco swore every time after he pulled the slot lever.

After twenty minutes, I found a restaurant that served noodles. Ultimately, it didn't matter what I ate since I still had no taste buds. *I wish I had those guys stop at the market to get better food for the children though.* My left leg now throbbed up to my hip as I walked. I had to keep leaning on my right foot. There were multiple elevators, and some went to the next building across the way. I got out the piece of paper Paul had given me with my room number. But it didn't exist on these elevators. I knew I was in trouble because shock still permeated my brain, overlaying me into more confusion from the noisy chaos. My mind whirled around like a carousel. My sporadic breathing forced me to stand against a wall not to faint. I couldn't focus on the elevator numbers to study their sequences. Sobs centered in my throat. A teenage couple, arms around each other, strolled past but didn't notice me.

An elderly attendant turned the corner, and I limped to him. Tears poured onto my blouse and my voice shrill. "I'm lost! I am registered at the casino hotel under a pseudonym because I'm Soorya Townley, the mother of the murdered Charla Mack."

So much for concealment. The employee looked straight ahead. He held a finger up as if to say, "One moment" walked away, and dialed his cell. After a long while, he came closer. "Ma'am, I think I know where you are."

I wanted to fall to the floor screaming, *Thank you!* But I cried hysterically instead. My nose ran and as I looked down, I realized I'd somehow cut my forearm and it was bleeding.

The attendant guided me to another elevator, and I crossed my fingers in hope. He escorted me to my door. "Here you are. You are in the wrong section," he said without emotion, then left without looking back. His lack of communication made me feel even more paranoid, knowing I had blown the secret cover by possibly letting the entire hotel know my identity.

After opening the door, I rushed to the bathroom and locked the door. At the sink I stared at my face. *What if this guy was corrupt and made a call to a real kidnapper, and now they knew where we were?*

Lisa and her two daughters, Jamie and Allie, knocked on the door. Before Lisa could speak, I flew into her arms. "I'm beyond relieved you're here." She hugged me back tightly. "I'm glad to see you, too."

The girls and I embraced. "Soorya, I'm just so sick about Charla ..." Allie, Lisa's oldest daughter, said, rubbing her eyes.

"I know, honey. I'm sick too. This is horrible."

Jamie asked, "Why did he do it?"

"None of us have any idea."

Just then, Christopher and Geni arrived with Erika.

"Christopher, how did you get Erika?"

"Lanny walked in right when we arrived downstairs."

"Fantastic."

After a loving embrace, Christopher said, "Lisa, we aren't staying here as we are with my dad, so you guys will have more room for yourselves."

Lisa sighed. "Your mom told me on the phone about Andrea. So tragic and how weird that she died the same morning as Charla."

"We have arrived in a bizarre land, Chris." (I thought it fitting to say again since Andrea had been a nun.) Hail Mary to Andrea.

I watched the girls as the adults talked. They held hands, as they walked toward the other room.

After Christopher and Geni left, I said, "Lisa, I'm feeling caged here. Did you take a taxi or rent a car?"

"I took a taxi."

"Okay, so we are car-less."

Lisa asked, "Why don't we just order room service and play games with the girls?"

"That's the best solution. I do better in smaller hotels, as walking through gigantic complexes is too overwhelming."

I didn't mention my breakdown with the attendant. Usually, the girls cheered at ordering room service. Now, all three sat saying nothing while sitting on the bed. Allie's face was expressionless as her finger rubbed the edge of a pillow back and forth. Erika dangled her leg on the side of the mattress while looking off into the distance. Jamie reached for a tissue on the nightstand. After Lisa ordered food, the girls went off to the adjacent room to be on their own. Lisa and I closed the door between them.

We sat on chairs across from each other as we went over the next day's arrangements. I looked up for a second and behind Lisa, on the back wall, I saw Charla clearly in a white form. Even though she was a filmy essence, she appeared more human. She was smiling and holding a baby wrapped in a blanket also made of white light.

"Oh, dear God, Lisa, it's Charla!"

Chapter 12
The Family Circus

The surprising appearance of Charla made me yell just loud enough to startle Lisa. I didn't want the girls to hear. "She's really and truly here, right behind you. Oh, my darling, Charla!"

Lisa's eyes looked at all areas along the middle wall. "Is she saying anything? What is she doing?"

"Not sure. Let me focus."

It thrilled me to see Charla again and content. I was apprehensive to walk any closer, afraid she might disappear.

"Charla's holding a baby, and there seems to be something important she wants to communicate. I'm getting the impression she somehow gave birth on the other side or that the child had been hers before she came to Earth. Or, somehow this baby is symbolic of something. Whatever Charla is saying, it's important. She *really* wants me to get information about this baby! But more thrilling for me is that she's happy!"

Indescribable feelings about being on the razor's edge between sorrow and joy took my heart over. "Hold on—she communicated that time, in her dimension, differs from here."

I had the same feeling when Charla had been playing with the lights at Anne Savage's house: there was no fooling around for Charla. No dwelling inside the garage where she spent her last dying moments.

There were no words to express how wonderful it was to see my former daughter.

Lisa's eyes watered.

"I can only imagine what you're going through. You and Charla were so close."

"I know. I'm destroyed by this. Is she still there—on the wall? I wish I could see her—even just once!"

"Yes, she's still there holding that baby … it's about a month old. I can't tell what sex it is."

Yet as I spoke, Charla began fading away, and then she left. The specks of imperfections on the wall appeared again. I wondered if Lisa believed me.

We all went to bed soon thereafter. I lay awake thinking about two extremes: Charla's new life, and worrying about viewing the cosmetically enhanced body of earth-Charla the following day.

♦

At 8:30 am, Paul called from the lobby. Once I settled into his car, he said, "I don't think you guys should let the children see Charla. It's more for adults, and it's terrible for children. It could traumatize them for life."

Lisa followed in a taxi with the girls. As we drove, I rehashed his words. I believed him. But then I feared that Erika, Jamie, and Allie might resent us later for not having the opportunity to say goodbye to Charla—like somehow, she'd just disappeared. This decision was life-altering; the consequences of my choice would be like permanent glue, sealed to everyone's fate.

I decided they would see her. Their innocence had already ruptured, and I feared that not having a chance to say goodbye to her might impact them more. And what was worse—knowing a father (or 'Uncle Darren') had murdered your beloved mother (or 'Auntie') or viewing the dead body? Lisa supported my decision.

As we entered the viewing room at Mountain View Mortuary, a small, nondescript auditorium, one of Charla's friends leaned over her casket, sobbing. He turned and saw us, and quietly slipped into the back of the room, He bowed his head against a chair and kept weeping. No one from the Mack family was present.

Allie startled me. "Wow, she looks terrible!"

Jamie said nothing but quietly cried next to Allie. Erika's eyes remained dry as she stared at her mother. Erika had not cried around me since I'd arrived in Reno. The girls stood beside Charla's body for twenty minutes. I sat a few rows away next to Lisa. My now familiar numbness crept in; I was floating outside somewhere again.

Lisa got up to say goodbye to her dear friend. Watching her bend over Charla, I froze further into the snow of sorrow.

Having seen my daughter's wounds the day before was enough. I didn't need to spend time with her again, especially now in front of the children. Especially after seeing her the night before in another dimension radiating light and happy with her baby. Thirty-nine years prior, I had brought her to earth through my womb. Now her spirit had been moved by force to another source. I had no choice but to release these few pounds of bones and flesh, which would become nothing more than dust.

The girls surprised me; they were graceful. After they looked at Charla and talked about her to each other, they sat down in a pew. All three held hands. Since they were doing so well, I walked to the top of the auditorium to greet a few of Charla's friends. My mother and Aunt Jackie appeared in the doorway and trailing behind them were my three cousins. All stood in a half-circle around Charla's casket. My hard-of-hearing mother screamed in her deep Kentucky drawl, "Soorya, this is *not* Charla!"

My mom's voice sounded as if on a microphone. Her reaction mortified me. Since I was in the back of the auditorium, I couldn't walk down fast enough to get her to stop. She kept repeating the same words. "Soorya! This person is not Charla!"

The room stopped in stillness.

I wondered what our children thought. Lisa rushed over to me. "Let's get the girls out of here."

"I agree." It terrified me she would traumatize them further and maybe others.

As my mother kept repeating the same words, I pretended not to hear her and didn't react. I felt terrible ignoring her, but I couldn't deal with her trauma on top of my own and the children's.

Lisa escorted the girls to the exit, and I signaled to her I'd be right there. Approaching my mom, I patted her shoulder and gave her a look of compassion. I spoke firmly into her ear. "Mom, it *is* Charla. She's had a violent death, and it's made her look different."

I didn't know if my words were accurate, but I had to calm her nerves. She wasn't wrong, though. Charla looked *nothing* like before.

Before, she was a vivacious, beautiful thirty-nine-year-old woman in the prime of her life. Now, she was desiccated, and shriveled. Makeup can't hide death.

I gave my mom a tender hug and told her to come by the hotel afterward. She looked as thrown off as I'd ever seen her—hair greasy and frail with bloodshot eyes. Despite me calming her, she kept pacing back and forth with loud mutterings, until my cousins gave me the "look" they'd take care of her.

I left as fast as I could to join Erika in the car. As we drove away, Erika exclaimed, "Boy, when I die, I'm going to get someone better to do my makeup than the guy who did hers. She looked terrible."

There are no dictionary definitions for "post parlor laughter" but Erika's comment broke the tension. We all laughed in unison as I unclenched my hands. I was grateful that the girls saw Charla merely having a lousy makeup procedure and not that her daddy had physically traumatized her mommy to the point she looked like a stranger. It also was remarkable that we could joke.

We ordered room service once we arrived at the hotel, and the girls gobbled down the sandwiches and French fries as soon as it arrived. There was a knock on the hotel door. My mother, Aunt Jackie, and first cousins Linda, and Charla, whom I'd named my Cha Cha after, had arrived for a visit.

Linda said, "I like that you guys are on the twelfth floor because the view here is incredible."

I nodded. "I know. Reno is one of the most beautiful cities in America."

The large picture windows in both rooms overlooked the vastness of the Sierra Nevada mountains. Clouds stretched across a clear blue sky that seemed to reach up to heaven.

Obviously, the view would have been more inspiring if tragedy had not crushed our spirits.

"Mom, come sit over here." I patted a dent in the pillow beside me on the bed. Aunt Jackie joined me on the other side.

My mother shrugged as she walked over. It seemed she had something to say again.

My cousins sprawled on the floor as my mom, and aunt squirmed on the bed. Jamie and Allie curled up on the floor. Erika, who had been in the bathroom, walked in. "Hi, everybody. I'd like to take you through an exercise."

"That's so sweet," I said. "What is it?"

I would have admitted to my therapist friends it didn't seem right that Erika occurred so commanding and centered. I knew she had to be out of touch with her feelings. But the current of life was moving too fast now to pause and help even an emotionally wounded child.

"All of you—close your eyes and take a deep breath." Erika waited a few seconds, saying nothing.

"Take another breath. Feel it seep through your body. Keep letting go of any sad or bad feelings as you breathe." She waited for a full minute. "Next, imagine you are in some kind of beautiful place," Erika's voice soothed. "See green moss around a massive tree beside you. The sky is blue and you are lying on a blanket underneath. There's a cool breeze. As you almost fall asleep, a giant panda bear waves as he passes by. He has soft and fuzzy fur and he smiles at you. Now take a deeper breath. As soon as the panda leaves, a gentle black bear mother with five cubs trots near you in a straight line."

Erika paused and added, "Take another deep breath. Let go of anything bothering you. The bear is happy, and she will not hurt you."

Erika astounded me with how articulate her story was and how composed her voice became as she shared. I realized Charla must have taught her that exercise to get to sleep. I wanted to fall into a dreamy state and join her words, but my mother stirred behind me, putting me on alert. I knew Erika's exercise befuddled her.

True to my paranoia, my mom belted, "Damn it, honey, I can't hear you, Erika.

"This is silly, Erika. I don't know why you are making us do all this. Soorya, why is she taking over?"

As if the day hadn't been stressful enough, my mother was now shutting Erika down in what could have been a sublime moment of beauty and togetherness. My sadness for Erika saturated my heart.

My mother's lack of sensitivity brought back memories of how she used to put me down for being creative as a child. Even when I'd won an art contest and my drawing was displayed on a public window in the center of town, she never went to look at it or praised me. Memories of not being acknowledged and only put down instead rushed through my head. I opened my mouth to scream, "Shut up!" Instead, I muttered, "Mom, it's just for a little while." I reached over and rubbed her hand. It didn't help.

My mother's impatience now erupted like a squawking saxophone. "Honey, Erika, this is enough! The adults need to visit now and not play this silly game!"

Erika's soft voice soothed. "Okay, everyone, imagine the bear has passed you by, and you feel calm and peaceful. Take one more breath and let your shoulders release. Please open your eyes."

I craved to leave with the bear. Erika had taken me out somewhere beyond this plane, but my mother's temper had pushed us all into some junkyard.

I approached the window to calm myself by looking at the mountains following my mother's indelicate outburst. A pink hue crested the highest peak.

In past years, this behavior would have provoked a long letter from me explaining my point of view. But all of that was over now. It would only take time away from Erika.

But my formerly chain-smoking, still alcoholic, hillbilly mother, who was raised in a two-room shack in Harlan County, Kentucky coal country, wasn't done. "Gosh, Soorya! Don't get near that window! Darren could be out there with a sharpshooter and he'll kill you right now!"

I walked over to my mother and said firmly in her ear, "Mom, stop it. You're scaring the children."

My cousins Charla and Linda took the cue to move the girls to the next room. They grabbed some books and closed the annexed door.

My mother's next words were still too loud: "He's out there, that son of a bitch, and he's going to kill us too!"

I couldn't tell if I'd lost control or gained it as I firmly placed my hand on my mother's shoulder and squeezed it hard. It was the most aggressive physical act I'd ever done to her. This time, I locked my piercing eyes onto hers. "Stop it now."

My mother shook her head. "My land, I think it's time for me to go home—back to Arizona."

"Maybe that would be good."

I felt awful that my mother would leave so soon, and with me disciplining her, especially with her not having the slightest idea why she had upset me. It was all about her. Nothing had changed since my childhood, and her behavior reminded me of the main reason I'd moved out on my own at sixteen. She had never been sensitive when I needed comforting.

My mom walked over to the closet door knob and grabbed her hanging purse. My cousins lead her outside into the hallway. "Soorya," my cousin Linda turned with wide eyes, "We're going to take Polly back to her room." My mother huddled next to them and turned her back on me. I was grateful Lisa hadn't been there. But the girls had heard it all.

After our brief goodbyes, Linda looked back and blew me a kiss and mouthed, "I'm sorry…" I shut the hotel door and studied the wall where my daughter had shone the night before. *Charla, did you see all that?* I imagined she understood more than I did.

Jamie came back into the room and cracked a smile. "Geez, families can be so weird." Those were the most astute words I would hear for months.

Chapter 13
What Arises and Falls at Funerals

June 21, 2006

It was Wednesday, the devastating day. The day of the memorial service and burial of our Charla.

While Lisa took the girls to the airport and waited for her husband, Gil, to arrive, I left early for the mortuary to set up the tribute brochures for arriving guests. The funeral parlor offered to print them, including a gorgeous photo of Charla holding Erika.

I had asked Dr. Liesa Leggett Garcia, the minister from the Center for Spiritual Living, to conduct the service. Her church was nondenominational and in alignment with my daughter's beliefs. I knew my Pentecostal Christian family would not be overjoyed because, to them, the service would be heathen. Either you focused on Jesus and the Bible, or you wouldn't get into heaven and you were a sinner. I dreaded their disappointment. Charla had never revealed to the rest of our family what she believed in. I marveled at how incredible it was that many of us have all these buttoned-up postures to conceal and protect ourselves so we never disturb our family tribal beliefs.

As people filled the chapel, it surprised and gladdened me that Charla's friends arrived, especially from California and Texas. Relatives I hadn't seen in years came. My emotional numbness reinstated itself, though, and I could barely acknowledge anyone. One of Charla's former boyfriends, Scott Hobbs, a California Highway Patrol Officer and the man I wish she would have married, filed in weeping.

I looked around the room and was happy to see my mother, who thankfully did not drive back to Arizona in haste. My cousins had calmed her, and she was front row center, quietly sitting on one of the padded chairs.

There was a stage at the front of the large room. Frosted windows in the back brought in light, but not so anyone could peer in. The press had asked to be present, but I refused them entrance. They gathered outside with cameras.

Reverend Liesa arrived. I reached my hand out to shake hers. "Thank you again for doing this. You are kind enough to come out at the last minute."

"No problem, Soorya. Is there something you'd like me to say in particular?"

I had attended Reverend Liesa's church a few times and taken Erika. Now, my mind was blank. I hadn't thought of composing my thoughts. "Honestly, I can't think of anything. You always give great sermons. I'll leave it up to you. I've decided after your talk to open the microphone to anyone who wants to share."

Reverend Liesa stepped back and raised her eyebrows. "Really? Are you positive you want to do that?"

The air suffocated. I leaned back against the wall for support. The same whirl of confusion as I had about the children viewing Charla's body hit me.

"Some … some people may need to express their sorrow," I stuttered.

"Good luck. Often it's not … not the best choice to do that though."

A feeling of acid rose in my throat.

"I'll take a chance and see how it goes. Could you mention Jesus for my family, though?"

"Sure, of course."

I sat near the front with my son and Genicia. I looked over at Joan with Lanny; dressed in rich colors of emerald green, she looked beautiful. Lanny in slacks was weeping again. All I could think of was we had been a family and how tragic this was for us all.

"We are gathered here to honor Charla, mother, daughter, friend. All who knew her loved her. Charla was full of joy and made others feel that joy through her."

Reverend Liesa shared about how Charla had ascended to heaven. I realized, sadly, I should have written something, but I was too far gone and too full of other people's chaos to even think of it.

"The holy ones are greeting Charla, and she will forever be at one with Creation."

Reverend Liesa's expressions were beautiful, but my mother and Aunt Jackie were unsettled. They whispered to each other and made low comments under her breaths that I was sure others could hear a row away.

My Aunt Jackie's "Lord have mercy" rang out.

Finally, Reverend Liesa said, "Charla is with Jesus."

I sighed in relief, hoping my family thought Charla was "saved." Lisa's eyes were wet, and her clasped hands trembled. I reached over and placed my hand over both of hers. Chandra whispered, "Charla was one of the most delightful people I've ever met. I will forever be altered by knowing her. Thank you for being her mother."

Christine Libert, who had written the quote to the Reno Gazette-Journal about how Amanda Robb had trashed Charla, spoke. Her voice was rich and filled with heartfelt stories. She said she had a list of poignant things to mention she had learned from Charla. "Charla taught me so much. Her aliveness, her enthusiasm, and kindness—her willingness to be generous at any moment changed my life."

My ex-husband, Robert, Charla's stepfather, and Christopher's dad, spoke next. "Charla was the sweetest child. She was always mannered, and I never felt the need to discipline her. Charla was giving and loving and spent hours taking care of my dog. She was like a small adult in a child's body."

Many people sobbed openly. I was so numb I could barely be present. My mind drifted amongst the audience with the realization that this was it. This funeral meant Charla's body would leave soon.

James, Charla's half-brother from their father's second marriage, approached the podium. James laughingly spoke about how much fun Charla had been as a half-sister. "On my twenty-first birthday, Charla took me to a strip joint, and I saw naked women on stage. It was the wildest experience I've ever had."

My mouth fell open, and disbelief took over. Having Erika, Jamie, and Allie in the room made it worse. How could he talk like that in front of the children—let alone about Charla?

I thought of those canes with hooks used in Vaudeville to grab awful actors off the stage. I yearned for that cane to drag James away. I knew if I spoke out to say "Please stop," it would embarrass both him and his family. I imagined hiding inside the stall of the bathroom. Just as I got up to stop him, he finished. But not before he spilled another story about a strip bar. He now set a tone of disappointment inside of me that I couldn't throw off. I realized his act was the folly of youth. The reverend had been correct.

It got worse. Mel Laub, a longtime friend of the Mack family and prominent Reno attorney whose name was plastered on large billboards across the city, was seated next to Joan Mack. He rose to speak. Since Mel had been Joan's friend for decades, I figured he would say something brief, polite, and kind, and sit down. Instead, Mel leaned into the podium and paused to look around the room. "See-e-e. There's no tension between the two families!" His voice and smiling face were as cheerful as if at a birthday party. He leaned further toward the audience. I imagined him talking to convince a jury.

I mentally screamed. Mel even mentioning "tension" brought tension! *How dare he bring that up?* As if my frustration with James hadn't been enough, now Mel made it messier.

"Everything is lovely between the two families." Then he had the nerve to add while giggling, "Soorya is my massage therapist."

Why would he say that? I had only worked on him twice while visiting Charla to be nice. I was a bull stuck by a matador, and the searing pain was all I could feel. I suddenly remembered an issue with him when I had called to ask a legal question before I found Egan Walker. His first words to me were within two days of Charla dying, "Oh, that was terrible how

Charla tried to get all of Darren's money in the divorce fight. She shouldn't have done that." I said nothing but realized he'd been groomed by Darren's hateful fabrications.

Lanny was the only person who softened me as all he did was quietly cry.

When the service was over, I walked over to Reverend Liesa. "You were right. I should have monitored what people would talk about."

"It's tough to know who will go off the deep end telling inappropriate stories."

We both shook our heads. "This too will pass."

The meet-and-greet in the hallway began without me. Still too overwhelmed to talk to anyone, I remained sitting. Several of Charla's friends handed out the brochures. I finally walked over to Charla's out-of-state visitors, but after the first two people, I slipped away and went back to the funeral parlor, sat in a chair, and placed my head down.

The funeral director approached me. "Ms. Townley, it's time to lay Charla to rest."

"Oh right," I mumbled. I'd forgotten that would even occur.

The director made the announcement for all the guests to follow. My body was a scattered wind tunnel of particles.

Lisa, Erika, and her daughters piled into Gil's rental car, and I went solo with the guards. Our drive was short, but as we wound past other graves the abrupt sounds of trucks traveling along the busy Virginia Street made continuous sharp jarring noises as they hit potholes, which made me wince.

We arrived at a spot with an open pit. Two men stood ready to lower the coffin.

I don't remember who was there. I even forgot about Erika. She might have walked over to her siblings, Elise and Jory. My mind felt the closest to not existing as anything I'd ever experienced. Somehow, I stood with the crowd. I never thought to seek my mother, cousins, or aunt. I forgot about Chris and Geni. If a pin had struck me, I doubt I would have felt it.

After the eulogy and prayer by Reverend Liesa, the men tightened several straps on the casket. Charla's former boyfriends assisted in carrying it. As the men lowered her body into the pit, they lowered something of me as well. Liesa said another prayer. "Father, Mother God, be with our dear Charla. As we become dust, so do we also become star bodies. Charla has moved on to her higher divine dwelling."

Even though the universe had given me the ultimate present of seeing Charla's spirit alive and happy on the wall, as well as greeting her in space the first night of her death, still, the stark reality hit that she was no longer here to raise her daughter, be my daughter or to be a friend. She wouldn't be a granddaughter for my parents to adore. She wouldn't *be* with us, and that was what counted now. Both realities existed: One would return to dirt and the other to spirit. But it left nothing for those of us on earth.

This was the most horrible day of my life.

It was even worse than when I first learned of her death. Perhaps because shock had enveloped me, and I'd hoped that the police were wrong. But her burial ritual, with each shoveled dirt that followed, threw away every dream I envisioned for my precious daughter. I internally said a prayer. "For anyone going through grief in the world, anyone who experiences the death of a child or a beloved, I wish them great courage, and universal love, always and forever."

I staggered toward the guards. Erika came from somewhere. "Grandma Joan asked if I could stay with her tonight. What do you think?"

"Sure, honey, if you want to."

Lanny appeared. "Soorya, I believe the danger is over concerning Erika, so starting now, I'm letting go of the guards."

Despite my grief and devastation, I smirked. A mere twenty-four hours later, Erika was home free, safe, and no longer in danger. The final act of the circus shit show.

Lanny left with Erika, and it was best I didn't have to care for her that night; my bankrupted body had already settled into an exhausted abyss. Lisa and her family would stay in another hotel for the night together. Christopher and Geni drove off to mourn his stepmother with his dad.

For the first time since arriving in Reno, I was alone. And I needed it.

Once the guards dropped me off at the hotel, I brushed my teeth and could barely remove my clothes. Instead, I slipped into bed, without my nightgown, pulled the covers over my head, and fell into a coma-like sleep.

The next morning, I remembered that I'd left all my condolence cards from Charla's friends in the back of the guard's rental car. I called Paul. He answered, "We turned that car in. I'll call and see if the rental company found them."

"Wow, I hope so because someone bought me a massage session at some spa place, but I didn't catch their name or the spa name."

"I'll see what I can do."

Paul called an hour later. "No one found the cards—I'm sorry."

"But I can never thank those friends or have that body work ..." My voice was shrill. "I can't write thank-you notes to the other people who sent me best wishes. How could no one have turned them in?"

"I'm not sure."

After we hung up, I remembered people had given me cash inside those cards as well.

I sat while wrenching sobs poured into my hands. I felt terrible that friends had generously laid out their money for my life, and it would go to waste, and they'd never have a clue if their gift brought me relief. More anger churned in my head because I knew if I had remained in our rental car, I would have kept those cards. The resentments of Anne Savage burned through me again. I was certain my mother and I would have smoothed over our upsets and taken walks in Charla's quiet neighborhood if we had the chance to stay together in that house. All the frustration and feelings of being overpowered by others gripped me like a home invasion. I sat with my arms around my body on the bed and rocked back and forth for a long time. *It's okay, sweetheart, you'll make it through.* Although, was it really possible to make it through with so much torment? Nine days had passed since this harrowing hell began. The most important question rang in my head like a ceaseless toll bell: Why couldn't I have died and my daughter lived?

Chapter 14
A Gathering. Moving In, Moving Out

June 22, 2006

The day after the funeral Ann Mudd put together a luncheon honoring Charla on a large horse ranch owned by John Harrah, the heir to the Harrah's casino fortune in the middle of Reno. Ann rented a house on the property.

I appreciated the towering trees paved along the road. Even in the massive summer heat, the green foliage looked vital and robust. The entire area had neatly trimmed lawns, manicured shrubs, and varieties of flowers ranging in rows of purple, orange, and yellow.

We parked, while women carried containers and bags from their cars up the stairs of a building. Lisa took our girls outside where other children played in the massive yard. I walked up the steps to see what was going on inside the house. The large high-ceilinged room with circular windows provided a view of the estate grounds. Several round tables were dressed with white tablecloths. The table looked festive, with several vases full of flowers and a beautiful rose tablecloth. The scene could have been a wedding.

Lisa approached me. "Hey, come outside. I want you to see something."

"Sure. I'm feeling stuffy here, anyway."

"It's Erika." She pointed.

Erika sat alone on a small grassy hill. I took a mental photo of her, which I thought would last for life: only eight years old. Erika's small body, her blue linen dress tucked above her knees with her hands folded on her lap, reminded me of a portrait I'd seen in a museum in Rome. The only difference was that a robe was draped over that little girl who had just experienced war. Erika hung her head the same. I knew my granddaughter's thoughts were torturing her—how could they not be?

Lisa shrugged. "I'm going to hang with her and see what's going on."

I watched them from afar. Charla had been an auntie to Lisa's children, and Lisa had been the same for Erika.

Eventually, other children came around, and Lisa walked back to me.

"Soorya," Lisa said, "Erika just told me, 'My daddy promised he'd never do anything to hurt me. But he's hurt me in the worst way he ever could—he took the one thing that was most precious to me—my mother.' I told Erika, 'I know, honey. What you are dealing with is just a terrible, horrible situation. It would be for anyone, but especially for you, since you are a child. We all loved your mother with all our hearts. I'm so terribly sorry.'" Lisa continued. "We hugged. I said everything I could think of to make her feel safe. I promised I would remain with her for years to come so we could weather this ordeal together."

"Thank you, Lisa. My heart aches for this child. But I know divinity has given her a gift, and it's you; you are also a gift to me."

We held hands and watched women coming and going, not speaking.

Lisa's daughters ran over. "Mom, we're hungry. Can you get us some food?"

"Yes, of course. Let's go in."

I thought we were all empty vessels, not knowing what to fill first.

Just as Lisa and her girls left for the buffet, Erika appeared next to me. "Honey, let's join everybody," I said.

"Okay."

As we climbed the stairs into the reception room, a woman around age thirty with dark hair rushed down the opposite way.

She reached out and extended a piece of candy to Erika. "No, she doesn't need that." I barked. "I'm going to give her some food right now."

My thoughts jarred into conflict. I did not know how my comment landed on someone who cared enough to come. I was also afraid I had disappointed Erika and sounded mean. My mood sank further, and I regretted reacting. My fear was that people would continually indulge Erika, feeling sorry for her, and we needed to keep things as regular as possible. So far, I was doing a lousy job of filling her mother's shoes. Charla would never have said a thing for a friend offering candy. She'd just privately roll her eyes to me and smile. Erika watched the other children interact with their mothers. "Sweetie, why don't you sit over there, and I'll get your favorite foods?"

"Okay, Grandma," she said in the most pitiful, tiny voice.

The Mack family was also present at the luncheon, and Mel Laub sat at their table. In the middle of the meal, as everyone was quietly eating and softly speaking to each other, the Mack table was full of laughter and glee. Mel Laub rose to entertain the Mack family women, including Joan, and began to do a fake strip tease for them, going so far as to unbuckle his belt. My son Christopher kept shaking his head, horrified at this fundamental lack of decorum and respect.

Mel's behavior made me remember when he'd asked me out on a date the year before while I was visiting Charla and Erika. He had me meet him at a restaurant. But when I got there and picked up the menu, and asked him what he was ordering, he said, "Oh I already ate."

That was off-putting and weird, but I ordered a pasta dish anyway. When it came he placed an elbow on the table to hold his chin while studying me. "Boy, you sure must be hungry the way you are eating all of that."

Embarrassed, I wondered if I seemed like a pig to him.

"Let's do a hot tub after this."

"I never do hot tubs on first dates."

Mel looked at his watch, stood up, threw some money on the table, and said, "Gotta go. Enjoy yourself." He walked out of the restaurant without another word.

I realized I had to make the rounds to say hello to my girlfriends who had driven from California. Once we were finished eating, someone brought out helium balloons and sent them off to honor Charla. I suddenly remembered I was now a mother again and had to get Erika home and settled. I said goodbye to everyone as the balloons disappeared into the air, along with my expectations of remembering all the names and faces I'd met.

Erika, Christopher, Genicia, and I departed the luncheon and drove to the temporary house offered by Ann Mudd and her parents, which was now ready for us. If someone had offered me a castle in France, it wouldn't have compared to the relief this space provided. The three-bedroom home was spotless and cozy on a quiet street with no cars. I couldn't believe our luck. The kindest, most generous people in Reno were stepping up to assist us.

As soon as we were settled. I made some lemonade and placed a puzzle on the dining room table. We sat down and began to piece it together. After a while, Erika opened up.

"Grandma, have the police found my dad yet?"

"No, honey, but they are in contact with him in Mexico."

"Will he go to prison?"

"The authorities will place him in the local jail, and then he'll have a trial."

"Do you know why my dad killed my mother?" Erika asked.

My heart sank. Even adults should not have to think of such a tragedy, and here was a

child struggling to understand.

I could barely speak. "We're all trying … to figure that out. It seems Darren had a lot of pent-up anger we didn't know about."

I could no longer bear to call Darren "your dad." I needed to be careful of what I said to not traumatize her further. Yet she'd already shown more sophistication than many adults I knew, including my mother.

After I tucked Erika in with her teddy bears, I fell asleep within seconds. Around 3 am, something bit my foot, hard. "Ouch!"

It was a cat—and not a content one. Apparently, I was in his bed. He hissed at me as his body remained inside the covers. I had to laugh, even though he scared me. Man, it's tough to get it right in life. The cat's anger lifted my humor a little. The next morning, I told Christopher, which seemed funny at the moment, "If it isn't a killer, it's a cat!"

We soon discovered that making irreverent comments provided relief. Dark jokes are often too precarious to share in public. But being alone together, we let loose. Chris said about Charla when Erika was asleep as the three of us huddled on the living room furniture, "Well, at least that's one less Christmas card to knock out."

To outsiders, the comment would have sounded awful, but it worked to help get us through yet another remorseful night.

That beloved house became an oasis and gave me the first feeling of comfort since arriving in Reno. I loved having Erika with us in an actual home. What loomed underneath, though, like a hungry reptilian on the prowl, was the miserable fact that Erika's mommy wasn't with us.

After four days, Erika had to leave us and return to Joan's. Christopher, Christopher, Geni, and I flew to LAX and then drove to Ventura. Early afternoon, I looked out at the gorgeous Reno terrain as the plane took off. I noted that it would be my third move back to that city. I had first landed there when I married Christopher's father forty years prior. Then I left when Robert and I divorced eight years later. My second move back occurred when Darren got spinal meningitis and nearly died in a Las Vegas hospital if Charla had not demanded that he get immediate medical attention. I stayed for six months in their cottage on the property to make raw food for him and nurse him back to health. Now, I was returning. Reno would not let me go.

Once off the plane and in Los Angeles, I walked into the central office of the Ventura apartment building, carrying a newspaper clipping of the murder to have proof that even though I'd only rented my apartment a couple of weeks prior, I had to back out of the lease. The office people understood and waived all fees; they had me sign papers to release me from my contract. I feared I'd have to fight them, but the process was the most uncomplicated legal action that occurred all year.

"Christopher, it's eerie saying goodbye to this apartment, especially since the candle and the photo of Charla are still sitting on the table."

"Mom, I know. All of this is beyond an explanation at this point."

"It's a relief that a lot of my stuff is still in boxes though. At least there isn't much to clean."

We walked into my spare room. "Mom, is this your music studio?"

"Yes, I was entering Dick Groves School of Music to be a recording engineer in September. I thought I would work on my music as a hobby. It's weird though, as now I don't have the slightest desire to be creative anymore."

Christopher and Geni left to buy some food, and I paced back and forth while looking at Charla's photo, calling clients and giving them the news that I was moving and could no longer be their massage therapist. It felt depressing and off to say such a permanent goodbye. I thought of the book title, "Been Down So Long Looks Like Up To Me."

Before leaving Los Angeles, I went to see a longtime client and friend, Alison Baumann, whose husband was the leader of the musical group Tangerine Dream, in her Malibu home at her request. To my amazement, she wrote me a check for $5,000 on the spot. Her gift gave me some financial room I needed to manage the transition to Reno.

After loading the truck, we were ready to turn in the keys to my former life and tackle a miserable ten-hour trip from Ventura to Reno with no air conditioning. Despite the whirlwind of life-altering events, I counted my blessings. In almost miraculous timing, I had a lawyer, a temporary house, and a new circle of friends. I was also grateful Joan Mack had allowed Erika to stay with us. I still hoped and longed for a partnership with her to make both of our lives bearable.

Erika had always adored her other grandmother. As we endured the long drive, I remembered a day when Erika chuckled at age three, "I think I love Grandma Joan more than you."

A few days later, she reversed her choice using a quiet voice, as if she sensed she might have hurt my feelings. It was sweet of Erika to include me, but I knew Erika preferred her other grandma, who she saw a lot more. She'd also said, "Grandma Joan is so-o-o cute."

My son startled me out of my thoughts. "Let's land the truck at the house for the night and not place anything in the storage unit until tomorrow."

Even though we were struggling, I knew every inch forward brought progress towards stability in Reno and satisfying the requirements needed to get custody of Erika. Nothing could stop me now.

Chapter 15
Courtrooms and Courting a Killer

Darren diminished his options as a fugitive in Mexico. Years past, he had relaxed and sunned himself with Charla, at the five-star, English-speaking resorts south of the border. Being on the run was a stark contrast. Darren would pay cash now. He was on the FBI's Ten Most Wanted list. An airline pilot had already recognized him from the *America's Most Wanted* TV show and called the police at the Melià Cabo Real Beach golf resort. The authorities missed apprehending him, though, because he only stayed long enough to give a woman employee the shivers by looking her up and down while she cleaned in the gym. This employee gave an interview to the *Reno Gazette-Journal,* expressing how creeped-out she'd felt when he wouldn't stop staring at her body.

The saga between Reno's District Attorney and Darren flared up in the news. Darren had previously emailed District Attorney Gammick requesting he became "My partner, in exposing corruption in the family court system, bringing the criminals to justice" (the criminals being Judge Charles Weller and Charla's attorney, Shawn Meador).

While on the lam, Darren wrote an email to Gammick: "I will be executed and soon become a statistic. But what can be accomplished here is to spark a change and stop the ongoing destruction of the family court industry. Then this tragedy will not be for [nothing]."

His requirements:

1. I will surrender only to Richard Gammick and who he wants to bring. I trust him.

I am unarmed exposed and will go peacefully.

2. I would like Mel Laub and Mike Laub to accompany Richard not as my attorneys but as my friends if Scott Freeman, Lawyer, Reno NV will come.

3. I will ask for the death penalty and want it agreed on prior to surrender. Even though I was defending myself from yet another attack from Charla, I am sure everyone [will] wan [t] someone to really pay for this. On another note if I had wanted Weller dead he would have been. I wanted him alive to have his corruption exposed and to get out what is really coming to him as well as the criminal Shawn Meador.

4. I want to see my family and children if they will see me.

5. Since I am stipulating the death penalty I want it done in 1 year so that I have time to have the truth of what has happened to me and others told.

6. I want a private cell until my execution.

7. I want access to a computer, printer, and internet, along with being able to see a writer regularly.

8. I want no prison and in exchange, I will not play the game and appeal, etc. A deal is a deal.

9. I want your word that you will support the truth getting exposed. Nothing more and nothing less.

Once Darren's lawyers spoke to him, they strongly advised him to stop talking to Gammick.

There was a problem. Darren failed to keep his promise of meeting Reno detectives at the town of Puerto Vallarta. After reconsidering, Darren now decided he was the actual victim. From Mexico, he contacted Fox News host Greta Van Susteren to see if he could arrange an online interview about how unfair life was treating him. He told her, "They want me to be the sacrificial lamb. They want the pleasure of executing me ... People have to understand that condemning any act in response to divorce court is like condemning us now for using violence with Osama [bin Laden]."

Van Susteren reported Darren called her enough times to overload her voicemail. She wouldn't interview him because of the specific demands he insisted on from her.

Two days later, Darren changed his mind and surrendered himself at midnight to Reno detectives at the Marriott Hotel in Puerto Vallarta. The police drove Darren to a nearby jail in the town of La Juntas. He later told a family member, "I had to spend the night on the filthy floor of the Mexican jail."

Darren Mack did not receive any of his demands on the flight home. Richard Gimmick recused himself from the case, since they had had luncheons together.

A shackled Darren arrived around 11 pm at the Reno International Airport, and police drove him to the Washoe County Jail. Detective Ronald Chalmers had flown in the back of the plane along with Darren and helped to get him booked.

Detective Chalmers let us know he had worked to open Darren up by sharing about his father, who was in prison for a life sentence for lewdness with a minor under fourteen, and also about his brother, a former heroin addict who eventually resolved his problems. Darren had cried when Chalmers talked about how his father's life had affected him and what Darren's son Jory would have to go through now. I thought it noteworthy he never wept about murdering the mother of his other child or just killing a human being.

Darren soon settled in at the Sparks County jail, a city next to Reno. Erika told me on the phone that Joan Mack dragged her there to see her father right away. I was livid. I had no recourse though.

My mind filled with horrible thoughts, thinking of what might go wrong with Erika being around her father and seeing other seedy prisoners. What if a man made a vulgar remark to her? What if she felt all the lack of love and repression in that jail or if the guards were horrible to the prisoners in front of her and that was more traumatizing?

Soon after arriving in Reno and once Erika was back with me, she seemed in good spirits. I focused instead on all the legal procedures required for me to gain custody of her, including the classes on child health and safety.

Joan Mack and I had our first custody hearing in the Washoe County Courthouse family courtroom, the same courtroom where Darren and Charla had waged a bitter battle over their divorce and custody of their daughter, the same courtroom where Judge Weller had ruled in favor of Charla, and nearly lost his life for it.

This custody fight wasn't my first. When my son Christopher was ten, my husband Robert filed his disputes to a bogus address. I never received notice to appear. When I didn't show up in court, his lawyer professed to the judge that I "didn't care" about my son and asked the judge to award Robert full custody. It took me two years to get him back. Now here I was again, eighteen years later, entrenched in another custody battle.

In the courtroom, police were present, as well as Social Service representatives and more lawyers than I imagined. Attorney Karen Sabo now represented Erika, appointed by the State of Nevada.

Earlier, as my family and I waited to enter the courtroom, we had watched Joan rush up to an outside reception area window where a clerk was. Since Joan was always pokey, (except when looking for Palace possessions), it unnerved me to see her rushing to the window. Joan loudly announced, "I want to adopt Erika."

The woman assured her through a glass window, "All legal processes channel through the proper order, and you will receive notice when it is the time to handle that."

I deadened in disappointment watching Joan because I knew I was involved in a fight I could not prevent; she would never let me have Erika.

Now in the courtroom, Joan and Lanny sat behind their three lawyers. No one looked our way. One attorney represented Darren. Egan whispered to me, "This is only a mediation."

The court did not expect the two of us to sit at the tables in front of a judge. Still feeling shy and mentally overwhelmed, it relieved me.

One of Darren's new lawyers, Scott Freeman, walked in. He had on a slick brown designer suit and shiny shoes. Freeman had formerly co-hosted the weekly television show, Lawyers, Guns & Money on KRNV-TV, an NBC Network affiliate. He represented Darren along with, but not present, David Chesnoff. Based out of Las Vegas, Chesnoff was famous for representing high-profile clients, including Mike Tyson and Martha Stewart. Through inside connections, we got the drift that Darren's family had already spent a million dollars just to begin the case. Darren had murdered Charla and attempted to kill Judge Weller because the judge had granted her $900,000 of their nine million savings.

Mediator and Juvenile Court Master Cindi-Elaine Heron walked into the room. Egan whispered to me she'd never conducted a hearing like this before. Our situation had never occurred in Reno, and this was a new process that the court used specifically for Erika's case.

Soon after, the courts implemented it as a matter of course.

While Freeman muttered to himself, Heron forced everyone else in the courtroom to switch gears. "Come to order," she commanded. "Are all parties represented by their lawyers?"

Joan's attorney spoke first.

"Yes, we are present."

Egan stood. "Your Honor, I am here for Soorya Townley, representing Erika Mack."

Much of the legalities addressed information about where Erika currently resided and how much time each party spent with her, etc. What Heron wanted to know was how Erika was doing emotionally. She first directed her question to Joan, who used her velvet voice, "Oh, she's *very* happy and she's great!" Joan sounded like they had all just arrived home from the Sesame Place vacation.

Heron peered down at her notes and paused. "Ms. Townley, how's Erika doing in your care?"

"Your Honor, it's been difficult. She tends to not share much, although she is doing the best she can under the circumstances. Everything is new to her. What I can say is that she's a strong girl, and she is attempting to adjust."

Heron announced she was giving me liberal custody rights, "but for now, Erika should stay with Mrs. Mack."

I had done everything Social Services required, but it wasn't enough. Aside from the fact I had strength as the maternal grandmother who deeply loved and wanted to save her granddaughter, I had many weaknesses. I did not live in Reno, nor own a home there. I had no ties there other than my now-dead daughter. I did not have a job. I had little in savings. Against me was Joan Mack, a prominent local businesswoman, lifelong resident of Reno, wealthy, surrounded by a large extended family and a coterie of high-paid lawyers. In my grief, in my shock, in my naiveté, I had thought that Joan would gracefully grant me custody and help me raise Erika as a partner. In reality, she was gearing up to bury me in legal bills and destroy whatever dignity remained in my shattered life. She thought she could break me. She was wrong.

After the hearing concluded, Christopher sat near the aisle and gestured for Scott Freeman to approach him. Christopher had signaled him as if to be friendly. When they shook hands, my son squeezed Freeman's hand tightly and fiercely whispered in his ear. Freeman squealed as he yanked his hand away. "Your Honor! Your Honor! This man is intimidating me!" All eyes turned towards Christopher, who put his hands up and sat down. Freeman rushed out of the courtroom.

As we walked outside and descended the courthouse steps a group of reporters approached us; we had determined that it would be best if our lawyer, Egan, spoke for us.

"Mr. Walker, how do you feel about Joan keeping custody?"

"Our focus is trying to calm the hurricane that's blowing around this child."

Egan's wise words made me thoughtful, yet inwardly, I was a mental mess wanting to protect Erika more.

Satisfied with Egan's response, the reporters melted away. As we walked to our cars, Karen Sabo approached me. "What you said was so honest. You didn't put on any airs compared to what Joan said."

I was still too stunned from court to think. "Thank you, Karen, I appreciate that."

I instinctively knew at least Erika was in capable hands to have this wonderful woman as her lawyer. As Karen walked away she paused and turned her head. "I just want you to know, Soorya, I'm a mother as well."

Later that night, I made a stir-fry in our temporary kitchen while Erika, Geni, and Chris watched a nature show. We'd picked up a newspaper and as the food simmered, I read that a reporter from the *Reno Gazette-Journal* wrote that Scott Freeman had approached them and said my son tried to "intimidate him" in court. Freeman stated, as Chris shook his hand, he had said, "How does it *feel* to defend a murderer?" I laughed inwardly. I loved that my son stood for his feelings of what integrity meant to him.

Christopher's cell rang. He got up and went outside to talk. When he came back, he beamed. "Mom, Ann called. She found a rental on Action Properties and it's near Erika's school. She thinks we should jump on it."

"So exciting. Let's go first thing tomorrow morning."

Our next step was to inspect this house, which was on a cul-de-sac. It was a three-bedroom, two-bath house next to the wetlands. We rushed through traffic to get to the rental office at 8:00 am and filled out the application. Within minutes of them checking my credit, they cleared me. I got the rental–at least I had good credit!

I smiled and mentally imagined my shoulders dropping a foot. “This is everything. I can create a home for Erika and be solid for court now!”

Geni’s face wasn’t smiling. She said, “I’m sorry to tell you this, but I have to return to Maryland to start the school year. But Christopher will stay here longer.”

I could hardly believe another major transition was occurring so fast. For a second I had felt excited about the rental. But now Geni… *If only there was a way to hold on to those you love, hold so tight that they were always with you …*

Chapter 16
The Girlfriend

July 2006

It is not an exaggeration to say my daughter was a packrat. When Christopher lifted the garage door at her rental house, we groaned in unison. Stacks of boxes filled the garage. Not even a motorbike would fit into that double car space. We also knew that Charla had rented a separate storage unit, which was also packed full. There were so many possessions because Charla and Darren, during their eight years of marriage, had together raised three children, Erika, and two of Darren's children from a previous marriage, in a two-story house in Washoe Valley, nestled between Reno and the Nevada state capitol, Carson City. That house was the central place to celebrate holidays for both families. Charla loved entertaining and having family and friends around. Charla felt happiest when surrounded by a roomful of family, and to be able to provide them food and drink and joy. Now, these material possessions, the only remnants remaining of a broken marriage and a destroyed life, were before us, and we had to move them out or be forced to pay another month's rent to the Savages. More importantly, a judge ordered me to store my daughter's furniture in a state-approved storage unit until the probate settled. But I could take the rest, which was a lot. I had just inherited her entire garage—along with all her personal possessions in the house.

But help was coming, including one of Christopher's close friends, who flew in from New York to help us move out of Charla's house. "Mom, guess what? This is Sushil, who you met once."

"You've got to be kidding … from New York, Sushi. I know Christopher calls you that. Thank you so, so much!"

"My pleasure. Where do I start?"

Sushil, Christopher, and Tony Mudd, Ann's former husband, moved boxes and furniture all day. As I watched Tony joke with Ann, I remembered Charla's mantra during her divorce fight with Darren: "If Demi Moore and Bruce Willis can be friends after divorcing, then so can we."

Nuggets of sadness dropped around me, watching helpers inside the kitchen dump in the trash what they deemed unnecessary. I retrieved pieces of Charla's stainless-steel mandolin and plastic coverings for her food dehydrator. I might have looked like a hoarder retrieving paper bags, rubber bands, and straws for Erika's lunches, but I hadn't found work yet and I wanted to save any amount of cash.

It impressed me that even Ann Mudd's parents Kathy and Gug, whose home we'd stayed at, arrived to help. The Puliz company in Reno graciously volunteered to unload my furniture for no charge into my new house. Then they came back and gathered Charla's possessions and dropped them off at the out-of-town storage unit. I suspected Ann Mudd had worked her magic again. I quickly saw who my real friends were.

I can't express enough how disheartening it was to watch the last part of Charla's life dissolve away including a gigantic banner she kept in her office, a quote from Maryann Williamson:

Our deepest fear is not that we are inadequate. Our deepest fear is that we are powerful beyond measure. It is our light, not our darkness, that most frightens us. We ask ourselves, who am I to be brilliant, gorgeous, talented, fabulous? Actually, who are you NOT to be? You are a child of God. Your playing small does not serve the world. There is nothing enlightened about shrinking so that other people won't feel insecure around you. We were born to make manifest the glory of God that is within us. It is not just in some of us, it is in everyone. And as we let our own light shine, we unconsciously give other people permission to do the same. As we are liberated from our own fear, our presence automatically liberates others.

This was my daughter's philosophy, and she practiced it as much as possible.

Ann had arranged a playdate for Erika for a few hours. I didn't want her to see her mommy's house erode away. She arrived late that afternoon. I left the television to be moved for last, so Erika could at least watch a show. She sat, with blank eyes, arms tucked, staring at the screen. Like at the funeral, there was no time for me to manage her feelings. The movers rushed so abruptly past us I could barely keep up with them. An hour later, they removed the TV. Erika said nothing. I thought of all the spoiled children who would have thrown a fit. Watching her tore parts of my heart that fell away like dead plants.

All of us cleaned the house as fast as we could since it had turned dark, and we wanted to leave forever. Even though my thoughts were in knots for this child, it felt reassuring to be breaking free of the Savages.

That night in our new house, I read Erika a story about a bunny. She smiled, and we both laughed because the bunny was mischievous. Afterward, I asked her how she felt.

"I'm okay, just sad."

Her voice was so pure-sounding, I would have clawed my way barefoot up a mountain in winter for her.

After Chris, Geni, and Erika were asleep. I went back into my new garage. I dreaded unpacking Charla's possessions. The entire garage was filled to the ceiling, exactly the same as Charla's rental had been. I couldn't fathom how I would get all of those belongings sorted. Her ten-foot-tall Frankenstein statute, for Halloween, stood to my right. As I looked into that cloth face with its decrepit painted eyes, I thought, *I really am in hell.*

The following morning, the phone rang. "Is this Soorya?" a female voice asked.

"Maybe."

Someone on the other end laughed nervously. "My name is Alecia Biddison. I'm a friend of Joan Mack's. She suggested I contact you because I'd like to have Erika come over for a sleepover. I have a little boy she's already met. They've hung out at Joan's. Erika was so charming with my son that I thought it would be nice for her to stay with us starting Friday through all day Sunday."

I held my breath. I'd never heard of this woman; something didn't click. "Alecia, thank you for the offer, and it sounds possible. I'll get back to you."

"Oh, wonderful. I'll plan meals."

Once off the phone, I wondered why this woman was already planning meals when I hadn't said yes. I dialed Joan. "Hey, a woman named Alecia called. She said you gave her my number and that you are friends. She wants Erika next weekend."

I grabbed a pen to write any details Joan would give me.

"She's a nice lady."

"So, you think Erika would have fun there to spend an entire weekend?"

While I smelled manipulation, I still felt it was important to get along with Joan and keep an open mind, even though Joan kept disappointing me. "Her little boy, Brandon, is a year old. It will be nice for both of them."

"Wow! He's a baby. That's a seven-year gap between them."

I wrote, BABY!!! on the pad.

Joan chuckled, "I think the age difference is fine. She can play with him like a doll."

"Yes, but if he cries a lot, that won't be a fun doll. Then it would be more like babysitting. Okay, well, someone's at the door."

No one was at the door, except Frankenstein in the garage.

My mind churned like making butter as I waited a day to call Alecia. Her determined energy resonated with pushiness.

"Alecia, how long have you known Joan—just curious."

"I met her recently after I met Darren."

"Oh, you became friends after the police picked Darren up?"

"Well, now that you put it that way … yes, that's how it went."

"Alecia, can I call you back? Someone's at the door."

No one was at the door. But my new sneaky line reminded me of a detective show. I was on the case.

I also thought maybe I should move Frankenstein to the porch. That way, he'd make me an honest woman.

What disconcerted me the most was that Joan had given Alecia my number without asking first. I called Joan back.

My voice was now firmer. "Joan, who is Alecia exactly? She's come out of nowhere."

"Alecia is a divorced woman and works from home. She's a close friend of Darren's." As soon as Joan mentioned Darren, her voice dripped velvet again.

"Oh, so she's someone he dated recently?"

"I'm not sure about their relationship." Joan's words hung like dirty laundry over my head.

"Okay, talk to you soon. I have to think about this." I didn't really have to think about it, just easing away from Joan.

"Great. See ya." Complicated Joan had mastered voice inflections to make you think she was *with* you. She'd learned how to pull customers in. Now I was one of them.

I called Pattie Haire, a friend of Lanny's, for years. Pattie had reached out to me after Charla died. She explained, "On the internet, Darren came across comments Alecia made about Weller. Darren wrote to her, and they clicked on their quest to have him unseated."

"Alecia and I aren't close," Pattie generously offered, "but … she shared some intimate details about how upset she was when Judge Weller gave her ex-husband joint custody of their son. She found an address in a small town in California to change residence for her custody case—Alecia faked living there instead of Nevada. The California judge overturned Weller's decision since it was too far for her husband to travel for every two-week exchange. So, the baby's father lost joint custody."

"But that's illegal!"

"I know. It's as illegal as hell, but she did it. To make it worse, she still wanted Weller gone and teamed up with Darren to make that happen. Their united front became their relationship. I have the impression that Alecia is over the moon for Darren, and has declared herself his girlfriend."

"Darren's using her."

"Soorya, all I know is that the same weekend Judge Weller's home flooded with bikers from an ad that someone placed to scare him and his wife, Alecia invited Darren to have dinner with her and meet her son. The two dated for about a month. One more thing about Alecia. She told the police that Darren asked if she'd like to go target practice one morning. That was the day before Darren murdered his wife and shot Judge Weller."

Pattie unraveled another story. "As soon as Darren surrendered to the police, Alecia visited him in jail and promised she'd look after Erika. I think Alecia desires to emerge as a centerpiece in his case and is now even helping the lawyers by typing material she's researched to use in his trial."

I dug my fingernails into my thigh and thanked Pattie before we hung up.

At lunch, Geni said, "I'm glad you know more details about this woman. As soon as you told me, I suspected Alecia wanted to set a trap to influence Erika to think Darren is innocent."

Several times I picked up the phone and dialed Alecia, but stopped. Finally, I grabbed my courage and reached her. "I don't think it's a good idea for Erika to spend time at your home."

She wailed. "But … but why? I've already planned everything. She'll have a good time."

"I think it's an awkward situation since you are such close friends with Darren."

"But, I … I can be a positive support for Erika to stay connected to her daddy, and also, Erika is free to talk about her mother any time she feels like it."

A cold chill ran through my head like ants darting from death. "Alecia, *of course* Erika should be able to talk about her mother any time she chooses—why would that even be a consideration for you to allow her to do that?"

"I mean, she is free to talk about her mother with me. I wouldn't stop that."

"You've already said enough for me to know you aren't the right fit for her."

Alecia whined, "I don't understand why you are backpedaling. I don't get it—why can't I have her?"

"I have to go." I didn't need a person at the door. This woman disgusted me.

I contacted Egan and explained the situation. Surprised, he took action right away.

"I'll write a letter about this for our court meeting next week to make sure there is a formal agreement that Joan will not trot Erika over to Miss Biddison's house or allow Miss Biddison to pick her up."

Three days later on Monday morning, at Joan's lawyer's office, Egan, Joan, and I sat in leather chairs. The pre-scheduled meeting was to smooth out any grievances Joan, or I had against each other. Egan explained my concerns about Alecia. Joan's lawyer, Kevin Ryan, sat across from us. I liked Kevin. He had walked over and reached out to shake my hand before our preliminary hearing and while Joan was in the restroom. "You are a worthy opponent, Ms. Townley. I'm honored to meet you."

I rubbed my palm across his thick mahogany desk as Joan asked about our concern with Alecia. "Why all the fuss?"

Egan leaned over and whispered in her ear. Whatever he said, Joan didn't ask another question.

She nodded her head slightly in agreement with our request, which startled me.

The meeting adjourned. Egan had such a way with words that he fixed the situation without more legal complications.

Once outside, I asked him, "What did you say to her?"

"I explained a child can't digest the murder of her mother, her father in jail for that murder, and then take on another layer that her father suddenly has a girlfriend. Joan seemed to understand, finally."

That same week, Social Services called and ordered me to come right away to a lab close by for a drug test. The voice on the phone said the State of Nevada made it a "standard procedure" in all custody cases. I dropped everything and went. While there, I called Egan to let him know. "Yes, I received a phone call before they called you. Both Lanny and Joan have to comply today as well."

A few days later, Egan called with the test results. "You and Joan passed, but Lanny failed. He registered positive for cocaine."

My mind drifted back to when Lanny stood up in the initial court and declared, "I want to co-parent with my mother to raise Erika."

"This changes everything." I laughed.

"Yes. It does."

Within a few hours, Social Services sent out an order stating they would not allow Lanny Mack alone in the same room with Erika.

Lanny created an emergency hearing to protest two days later. Joan's lawyers, Egan, and I settled into the courtroom used for our other hearings. Lanny accused the laboratory of colluding with Social Services and pulling one over on him, to be seen in such a terrible light.

"This is because of Darren. The authorities are out to trap me, too. They are out to hurt our family and to make me look dirty."

At home, I called Lisa in Los Angeles. "Hey, what does 'dirty' mean concerning drugs? I've never heard that expression."

"It's a common language that most addicts use."

"Oh, I get it. I could tell Joan had been infuriated at the meeting. She had crossed her arms more tightly than I've ever seen her while mumbling loudly under her breath, like my mom did when mad. She said, 'I can't believe Social Services would stoop so low as to frame my son. Lanny would never take drugs; this is not right.'"

I added, "Lisa, I can't imagine the State of Nevada would take a chance to have their license revoked, and create a scandal framing someone for a drug test. What would be in that for them?"

"Exactly. It's not like someone in a high political office is behind the scenes adjusting the state's chessboard. Lanny isn't even on the board."

The next custody exchange at Joan's house erupted into hostility. As soon as I saw her, she seethed. "I think *it's fine* for Lanny to drive Erika around and that court order is unfair, even ridiculous."

Joan wouldn't budge and refused to adhere to the new rule. When I picked Erika up at her home, Lanny was alone in the same room as Erika, while Joan was nowhere in sight. I knew Joan was testing me, but I was too tired to fight her. Lanny was a kind uncle, so I let the matter go and didn't report the issue to Social Services. I hoped that somehow, they would see my generosity as an olive branch. I kept counting how many times I kept silent, then gave up—I realized nothing I said or did would ever gain me points with the Macks.

♦

In late August, school started. Erika and I were lucky. Recognizing our plight, the private school's principal, Mary Levy, invited her to continue attending for free. Once I settled Erika into her first day of the new school year, I drove to court to hear the judge's *temporary* custody decision. It seemed an unreal situation to be in that area, since the back of that building was where Darren had shot the judge. My shoes were overly tight, but oops, too late to change. I limped from a blister, already hurting my heel.

The court assigned Judge John Iroz of the Sixth District for Erika Mack's custody case between Joan, Darren, and me. The entire gaggle of us, including police and a reporter from the press, stood as our judge entered from a door to the left into the small courtroom. I felt scared and unnerved just to be there. Egan reached over and squeezed my hand. "Don't worry," he whispered. "It's going to work out."

Within minutes, and before I realized what was occurring, the judge gave me temporary physical custody of Erika. He awarded Joan liberal visitation rights four days every other week. "This is typical of how divorce cases go," Egan whispered as he winked at me. *But this isn't a typical divorce case!*

Although elated at the judge's decision, I didn't want Joan getting so many days with Erika. I was fearful for Erika to be under the Mack family's influence, because they now openly declared to all that Darren was as innocent as a newborn baby and that he'd only killed Charla defending himself. I knew that the family would take Erika to the jailhouse to visit Darren.

Egan and I were the first to leave the courtroom. I went to the water dispenser while Egan waited for me near the elevator. Joan came over while I drank. "Soorya, I'd like to get together with you in person one of these days to tell you *our* side of the story."

A part of me would have loved out of perversity to have gone and listened to their "side," but I knew I'd end up screaming at them and it would turn ugly. My head suddenly felt as heavy as a bowling ball, but I lifted it anyway and nodded. I hurried over to Egan as fast as I could without running. He pushed the button for ground level. "Soorya, I know you're nervous about letting go of Erika eight days a month, but it will give you time to settle back into yourself, aside from always being in the mother's role. Plus, you can go have some fun if needed."

"I know. I realize that too. But I'm gripped with fear about them influencing Erika with their stories. I came here to protect her, and I'm afraid I'm not managing that."

"Children are resilient, and I think you'll be surprised at how well your granddaughter will thrive if given the love and care of her two grandmothers."

"I love how insightful you are, and I'm trusting you are right."

The judge decided; I had to move forward. Even though my pants were too tight, from yet another weight gain, I drove to a store and bought chocolate chip ice cream—I ate the entire pint sitting while grumbling in my car. Then I went back and bought a package of lemon cookies.

Too Soon, it was already Joan's week to have Erika. Since I was running errands close to her house, I thought I'd return the plastic containers she'd left at the school for lunches. The sidewalk next to her house afforded a view through a large window of her dining room where Joan, Lanny, and Alecia Biddenson huddled at the dining room table, talking so intently they didn't notice me passing.

Alecia had been in the military; she knew how to fight; she'd already used underhanded tactics in her custody case. I saw them as a cabal, which unnerved me even more—especially now that Alecia was free to influence Erika on Joan's time.

I thought of calling Alecia to be candid and reveal stories about how selfish Darren had been to my daughter. But I had too many other fires to put out other than to help the current girlfriend of Darren Mack.

Chapter 17
The Guardian Angel

My decade-long relationship with Joan Mack was now extinct. The beginning of the end occurred with Erika. She sometimes still liked to be wheeled around in a cart at the supermarket. Right when I lifted her and helped place her legs in the divided slot, she looked at me with her full-moon brown eyes. "Gramma Joan says she's in a battle with you over custody of me."

I paused to think by moving us next to the glass door of a freezer. For a second, I opened the cold door to shift the red heat of my upset. "Honey, I wouldn't call it a battle. We both just want what's best for you. I'm sure we will work through all our differences."

I was stunned that Joan was planting negative ideas in Erika's head. By now, I recognized this child's regular demeanor was a downtrodden face and hunched-over shoulders. I never dreamed Joan would drag her further into our chaos. During my spiritual conversations with this woman over the years, she had given me lofty words that spoke about her faith in God and life. I assumed she had a noble spirit. Maybe that had only been to impress me.

Even though, according to Joan, we were battling, I still held onto hope that a miracle would help us find a united comfort zone. My Native American friends taught during fireside gatherings that women are the salt of the earth, primal, and should always stick together.

Our relationship further plunged when I received a call the next morning from Chandra. We'd become friends and talked regularly. "Soorya, let's go to lunch today. I want to run something by you that's bothering me."

While we waited for our food at our favorite Thai restaurant, Chandra peeled through her purse. "Here it is—I've got some notes." She took a deep breath. "I've thought long and hard and decided it's your right to know. Joan asked me the morning after the murder if I'd like to co-parent with her to raise Erika."

"What? You're kidding?"

"I wish I were. Joan said that I could have Erika on the days she's too busy at the store and when she's out of town."

My elbow accidentally knocked over my glass of ice water. I used my napkin to sop up the mess while listening to Chandra.

"I told Joan, 'I think that is Soorya's rightful place. Charla wanted Soorya to raise Erika because she told me so.' We had several conversations about it."

"This is shocking. What was she thinking?"

"Apparently not about your feelings, or Erika's either. Because as time went by, Erika would wonder why you hadn't come forth to be with her."

The server arrived with some spring rolls. I couldn't hold my nervous laughter back, which was more of a defense mechanism. "I'm sorry—it's not you—it's … nothing surprises me at this point. Her two-face behavior is destructive. I'm crushed.

I'm nothing to that family. Would I be in the coin section of the pawn shop as a penny? Joan has a lot of nerve to go behind my back making those decisions. And the morning after the murder? Wow, she was even busier than I'd realized when her clothes looked so disheveled."

I added, "Egan found out Joan filed an affidavit with intent to have ownership over Charla's ring and watch from her house the day after her murder too. Now I hear she tried to get custody of Erika by aligning with you!"

"Look, even if you didn't exist, I can barely manage my three sons and be a decent wife, let alone take on the psychological impact of a child whose father murdered her mother."

Joan was a suitcase of secrets.

"What hurts me most though, is Joan's insistence on dragging Erika to the county jail. She has to be seeing a seedy side of life. It mars more of her innocence. She's not just visiting Darren with chains on his legs in a jumpsuit, but she's also seeing everything and everyone else. Jails are not for children; it's always about punishment."

"I agree."

After Chandra and I parted, I remembered what Erika said when I asked her questions about going to visit her father in jail; "I don't like going there, but Gramma Joan makes me."

I called Egan to see if I could limit Erika's visits to the jail. Egan said we could address the concern at the next court hearing. The courts still hadn't settled our final custody arrangements because neither of us had received our Social Services certifications.

Until then, I had no legal power.

Having exhausted all of his leave from work, Christopher secured a temporary government assignment with the U.S. Forest Service, which meant he couldn't help me on weekdays.

The following weekend, Erika had been at Joan's. When Joan brought Erika home Sunday evening, she came in with her instead of dropping her off curbside, as she normally did. I forced myself to greet her. I hugged Erika and noticed she had an angel pin on her shirt. It looked like real gold with emeralds around the head and crushed rubies on the body. "Honey, your pin is beautiful. Where did you get it?"

"Daddy gave it to me for an early Christmas present. Daddy says I am his guardian angel!" Erika gushed in her little girl's voice.

Joan turned her head, and I sensed a smile as she stood by the open door. The sun moved behind the nearby mountain, and a shadow shrouded her. I noted the darkness on her body and reminded myself to be careful and not to lash out. "It's beautiful."

Inwardly, I seethed. *Erika, if you are Darren's guardian angel, then he must be your big devil!*

This was one of hundreds, perhaps thousands, of tongue-biting moments where I could not express my angst, anger, and hurt. In the cat-box of hell, I had to scoop and remove all those fragmented balls of anguish. I was going to temper myself no matter what. My love for Erika was more important than my hate for Darren or his mother, although my issue wasn't just about love overcoming hate. It was also about a specific sensitivity for the deceased—her mother. To see the perpetrator manipulate the daughter of the victim, and for Joan to stand by and allow that to happen, was nothing short of profound injustice.

After Erika slept, I sat on the floor inside my walk-in closet. As I moved my shoes to the side, I couldn't stop the deep waves of wrenching sobs. How could a father take a sacred icon of an angel and announce to a child, after you butchered her mother, that you ordained her as your guardian angel? It was unbearable. Everything stable I had known before this seemed perverted, squished into new meanings because of one man's hateful actions. It broke me on the altar of humanity. I lost all hope.

The next day, and after I removed the pin from Erika's shirt, I called Lisa and complained.

"I bet Darren delivered it to upset you. He knows how spiritual you are."

"I don't know … What I do know is that Darren is about Darren, and Joan got that pin from the Palace for him. So, was it Joan or her son? Either way, it's messed up."

Lisa added, "Darren can't think far enough to realize placing the responsibility of being an angel on a little girl might harm her. Or maybe he doesn't care. I mean, he got rid of her mother, with her in the next room. For sure, he doesn't have enough sensitivity to recognize she shouldn't *have* to protect him, and that he doesn't deserve protection, especially from his child. He's so perverted."

I shuddered. "If someone killed Darren in prison, Erika might carry that guilt. Not being able to save him could set her up for more emotional pain. Thanks for your help, Lisa. I needed a sounding board."

I drove to Egan's office the next day to talk about the pin. Luckily, he had no clients and took me right in. "Soorya, I want you to know that Joan filed another negative affidavit against you and wants to have a court hearing to present all the reasons she thinks you shouldn't have Erika. She wants to advance our court schedule before you complete your requirements."

I was marinated in misery. So now that Darren was in the picture, suddenly Joan had so many grievances against me we needed to go to court before our hearing.

On the drive home, I played metal rock music full blast. Not true. I rode in silence with the window cracked and focused on traffic. Frightened about how much cash it would take to fight these humans, I wondered: *What if I wasn't a good enough make-shift mother to Erika? How can I manage all of this?*

Christopher came late from work, and Erka was already in bed. After I explained what occurred, he watched me bury the angel pin in the garden. I brought out a candle, lit it and sat on the lawn, and prayed over the spot.

"Please heavenly father, I ask that any intention made around this pin will never hurt Erika."

Christopher bowed his head. We later stood arm in arm. He said a prayer as well: "Heavenly Father and Mother, I ask that you grace my mother with the strength to endure all she has to during these trying times. I also ask that the murderer's mother, Joan, finds her compassion and that her son cannot do more evil mischief."

I once read that if you place a crystal, metal, or a jewel in dirt for a day or so, it removes any charge on it. I left the pin in the soil for weeks. Eventually, I placed it in a small box in the dresser under Charla's photo. I waited to see if Erika would ask for it, but she never did.

Chapter 18
Work and Divine Healing

I wasn't sure why Joan hadn't thought of enrolling Erika in a camp program for the rest of the summer, instead of assuming Chandra would just take over. All I knew was we both needed help caring for Erika during daylight hours. I continued driving her to camp, inside a wooded area. It was also easy traveling since it was around the corner from our house.

With more available time, I studied for my license exam required by the State of Nevada to work as a massage therapist. I also attended classes to complete all my coursework required by the Washoe County Department of Social Services. What lessened my annoyance was that Joan went to the evening sessions, and I didn't have to sit in the same room with her. The tension between us now felt like a wall of fire. I found the classes invaluable and thought all parents could benefit from the information.

The manager at Steamboat Hot Springs promised that as soon as I had my massage therapist license, she would hire me. It was close to Erika's school, and I could finish work and pick her up without problems. A church ran the spa; I crossed my fingers that the people had strong values and would be easy to work with.

In August, which seemed like a year had passed but in reality, only two months after Charla's death, I took the state board exam. During the test segment, one instructor said, "If you accidentally uncover your model's private parts, it is an immediate failure."

I was so nervous that I kept dropping my lotion bottle on the floor. This meant I had to take alcohol and wipe the bottle with a towel, which made for an awkward pause. One of the two judges asked me a technical question on anatomy. I couldn't remember and burst into tears, thinking I'd failed. I'd never been good at muscle memorization. But they smiled and handed me my test results. I received an 85%, which meant I passed! I was ecstatic.

All those hot, sweaty nights in July studying and thinking I would go mad from having to remember anatomy had paid off. One more obstacle out of my way. Driving home on the freeway, there were hardly any cars. I rolled down the window and screamed, "Thank God, Thank God! Thank God!" Terrified I wouldn't be able to support Erika or me, my elation pumped out like a gigantic party favor on New Year's Eve. It felt odd and out of sync to start from scratch in my career, as I'd been self-employed for almost three decades in Los Angeles and was at the top of my game there, with celebrity clients including Sting, Lily Tomlin, the Joan Rivers family, owners of record companies, movie producers, and many other notables. Now at age sixty, here I was, in an entry-level position working with kids fresh out of school. But I was grateful to have any job at all.

During the first week of Erika's school, I picked her up and, right away, she said she felt sick. I placed my hand on her head and she was hot. I put her to bed early and gave her vitamin C. She refused to go to school the next day. I kept her home, fed her soup, and propped up pillows under her legs as she watched TV. By that evening, she was coughing more. "Honey, if you aren't well by morning, I'm taking you to the doctor."

"Okay, Grandma," she said with a weak, throaty voice.

That night in my bed, I looked up and saw a form in white filmy gray light near the ceiling. I immediately knew it was Charla. She slowly floated toward the door, as if beckoning me. I followed, and she drifted into Erika's bedroom. I sat on the floor watching her as she lay beside Erika. Right away, she placed her right hand on Erika's forehead and then heart. My euphoria and yearning to hug her was overbearing, but I remained still the entire time—for about an hour. After that, she moved away and floated to the front door. Shyly, I walked near her to say goodbye. She stood at the door and appeared like a statue, yet there was also something holy happening, as she now emanated a brighter light internally. That said, her expression reminded me of someone forlorn, and not what I had imagined holy beings to appear like. I sensed she was expressing her empathy to me and that she understood better than I did what I was going through. After a minute, she faded away. I felt gobsmacked by the experience and barely slept afterward. All I could think about was sending her love.

By morning, when Erika awoke, she was completely well. She no longer had a sore throat and her fever was gone. "Grandma, may I go to school today?"

"Of course, honey."

I was astounded that Charla was able to heal her daughter from the other side. Even though I had been through the worst experience possible for any mother, I felt blessed to have felt Charla's presence again and grateful she had helped Erika.

I kept taking long walks to the wetlands, absorbing the beauty of the mountains and breathing in the fresh air. My daily life whiplashed between horror and the sublime. Every prayer I said that week was a thank you, for all the help I was receiving.

Chapter 19
Facing It All Alone

In October, Erika and I said our goodbyes to my precious Christopher, who had to return to Washington DC for his job. "Mom, I hate to leave you, but you are on your feet now."

"I'm going to miss you terribly."

"Uncle Christopher, I'll miss you too—a lot."

Erika's eyes filled with tears. Christopher lifted her off the ground for a hug. "I know, honey, but Geni and I will visit as soon as we can."

Erika and I were arm in arm and silent as we watched Christopher's plane fly away.

By now, life had forced me to be used to my loved one's leaving. This loss was the worst, though, as Christopher's departure felt like an appendage dropping. Yet, with mixed feelings, I was happy he was re-reuniting with Genicia, and she was excited for him to meet their new puppy named Teddy Bear.

A few days later, Joan and I went to court again since our custody agreement still wasn't final.

Our meeting was held in a massive room with twenty-five chairs arranged in a circle. It surprised me that so many people were present: Darren's attorney, Mark Wray, Joan's lawyer and mine, and, of course, Social Service representatives–even police officers. Joan and Lanny sat on the opposite side of the room. The space was so large I couldn't see their facial expressions.

Mack's lawyer, Mark Wray, announced, "Darren Mack is listening in from the Washoe County Jail."

Oh God—I'd forgotten he has the right to listen.

"Darren, can you hear me, okay? This is Mark."

"Yes, I can hear you clearly."

"Great. If you have any questions, I'll get back to you after a while."

"Thank you, Mark, and yes, I do have questions. I also want to acknowledge all the people in the room who have taken the time to make this meeting happen. Thank you for your efforts and who you are being in life to help my daughter."

Wanting to puke, I grimaced instead. This was Darren's jumbled jargon, a reflection of his former life as a Communication course leader for Landmark Education. In that role, he met my daughter, who designed flowers for restaurants and weddings; she also led a Landmark course in health and wellbeing and was being trained by Landmark's top leader. Darren seemed to be the perfect mate for Charla. Fit. Handsome. Wealthy. Into self-improvement. It was love at first sight. Landmark gave a dinner one night for all the course leaders and Charla was so enthralled with Darren that she quietly asked a team member if she could trade seats to sit next to Darren. She charmed him enough they went out afterward and stayed up until dawn talking. They were both hooked immediately. Charla flew to Reno regularly to be with Darren. She championed his efforts to gain custody over his small children from a previous failed marriage. He proposed, and they married on a May day in 1996 on the north shore of Lake Tahoe. Unseasonal snow fell outside. Charla had found her Prince Charming. But unlike a happy fairy tale, her Prince Charming murdered her, and I was left to sweep up the broken pieces of Charla's life.

At first, I admired Darren and trusted my daughter had finally found her mate, although, within a year, I had an uncomfortable feeling about him. The first time we went out for lunch together, he never looked me in the eye when we talked. Over food, I mentioned I had always wanted a golden locket to place my children's photos in. I asked him if they had those at the store and he said yes. I assumed he would bring me a locket on our next visit, but he never did in the decade I knew him. In fact, the opposite occurred. A client had gifted me with a ruby stone set in a necklace. I asked him if he would sell it for me to pay my bills when I was staying in their cottage after he had just recovered from Spinal Meningitis. The next month, I asked him "How's the sale going?" He said, "Oh, sorry, we lost that ruby."

He made it up to me by bartering a used Kirby vacuum cleaner from the pawn shop, but I suspected Darren got the better deal out of that trade since the vacuum was twenty years old. Now I wonder if the ruby had really gotten "lost."

Over time, Darren's narcissism became more pronounced. He was obsessed with bodybuilding, competing and winning a few body sculpting competitions. His discipline was impressive. He would wake at 4 am each morning to work out, and then work all day at the pawn shop. But he couldn't lift a finger at home to help Charla on their three-acre estate, not even to take out the garbage. Charla did everything, including plowing snow, building, painting Christmas yard decorations by hand, and managing contractors. Resentment built when Darren also ignored the children. Their worst fights were over him exposing the children to violent or sexually explicit movies when they were in the room. Charla would walk in and be enraged at his staring into the screen thoughtlessly while wide-eyed children watched as well. As Detective Chalmers had rightly surmised after spending only a short time with the shackled criminal on the plane flight back from Mexico, Darren believed he was the center of the universe.

Joan Mack had raised Darren this way. Wealthy children are often spoiled, but in the Mack household, the children, Darren and Lanny, were not only spoiled but were never held accountable for anything. As an adult, Darren's narcissism grew more pronounced. He was able to cloak his core character with multiple masks he wore for the outside world.

One mask was that of a hardworking entrepreneur, and he was. He not only preserved but also expanded the business his father had built, a business of vultures hawking the willingly pawned possessions of the desperate and broke.

A second mask was that of a teacher. Darren loved to feel puffed-up and important, wiser and cleverer than anyone in whatever room he stood in. He had a strong, powerful voice, and was able to weasel his way into Landmark Education's cadre of course leaders through his self-assured charisma. His most prized possession, in an office bereft of books, was a framed feather given to him by an Indian man and part of the northern Nevada Shoshone tribe. The man had taken his Communication course in LA and presented the feather to him with a surrounding audience. Darren displayed that feather with pride, as if it fostered some recognition as a wise man and a sage.

The third mask was that of a playboy. Darren loved sex and was a sex addict. It was what drove his bodybuilding. It was what drove him to make more money and gave his life a carnal purpose. If he forsook feasts and alcohol, he splurged on sex. It was his raison d'etre. It was also his downfall, the downfall of his family, and the fundamental reason for the death of my daughter.

When Charla refused to continue swinging with Darren, his mood turned sour and violent. While she was nursing Erika as an infant only a week old, he stormed into their bedroom and announced if she wouldn't swing with him he was divorcing her. Like many abused women, she hid her black eyes from friends and family, even a broken bone. She bore his aggressions and insults as long as she could, but ultimately, it was her daughter that mattered, and her dignity.

Darren promised Charla they could have a "friendly divorce" and he talked her into not obtaining a lawyer. "We will save tons of money," he said. Soon after, she visited her father at the pawn shop. Charla literally tripped over a file box on the floor. It spilled and as she bent down to pick the papers up, she discovered that Darren had hired a lawyer and had begun a divorce proceeding, with action to leave her penniless, despite years of devoted service to him as a wife, being a mother to his two children and bearing his third child. That same day she found Shawn Meador and filed for divorce. But the betrayal made her bitter and hurt her profoundly. Charla won the battle but lost the war when Darren took her life.

I was unwillingly drawn into this conflict, and planned to win the final war over Erika through love, instead of violence. Through righteousness, rather than with resources. Though truth, rather than conniving, demonic lies. And here again,

I was in a courtroom, confronted by the twisted tales of the Mack family.

Diane Wozinaic spoke about Erika's progress since the last hearing.

Suddenly, Lanny bounced out of his seat, with his arms flying up. "Jory flew back east to be in a shooting contest. He placed first! I think that's fantastic. We are very proud of him!"

The room took a long, dead pause.

Poor Lanny. He needs something to be proud of for his family. Not developed enough, he couldn't see how tacky and disgustingly inappropriate his words were.

I wanted someone to tell him to shut up. It was beyond embarrassing that he brought up shooting with guns while Judge Well's stitches were still healing. Finally, a voice from the back said brightly, "That's wonderful."

Heron asked, "Ms. Townley, how are you doing?"

"I'm getting settled. I also have a great desire to build a bridge of love between our two families."

Just like Lanny's comment about Jory's success, the room paused. No one was ready for my hippy-dippy enthusiasm. I wanted to slide under the floorboards. The awkward silence for me was even longer than Lanny's. Maybe because no one could say without sounding stupid, "That's wonderful."

Mark Wray broke in and inquired what Darren's questions were. "Thank you for asking, Mark. I appreciate it. I want to know if my parental rights are still in order?"

"Yes, Darren, they are intact."

Darren's voice exuded deep rich tones rolling like a Herculean wave in the water. "Again, I want to thank everyone in the room for all their efforts to help my daughter. I want to make sure everything is handled in a certain way, so she has the best opportunities possible, and I definitely want my mother to have custody."

That last comment felt like an attack on me.

Later, as Egan and I entered the street, my knees buckled. Egan reached over quickly and took my arm to balance me.

"I'm going to make sure we don't have another hearing like that."

"I agree. That was horrible!" I spoke louder than I meant to.

"There were too many people and too much for you to absorb. I'm also going to make sure Darren has limited talking time. I barely sat in my chair; I was livid over his comments."

Hearing Darren's voice, and that he had any right to speak and have any say in the destiny of the child whose mother he had murdered …

Chapter 20
Legal Crap and Crap Therapy

November, 2006

One day early in her school year, Erika's teacher, Jackie called and reported that Erika saw children whispering about her as she passed by during recess. On her lunch break, Erika asked the school principal, Mary, for a meeting with the students, which she arranged.

Once the students were seated, Erika asked them, "Is there anything you want to talk about?"

A few asked how she was doing.

"I'm fine. It's been hard, but I'm okay."

Another child asked about her father. Erika answered as honestly as she could that he was in jail, and yes, she had seen him. One child wanted to know more about Darren, and Erika answered as candidly as she could.

"Are there any more questions?"

Everyone remained silent or some shook their heads.

"From here on out, I ask that no one talks about this again. I want you all to let it all go."

Jackie was astounded at how calm and mature Erika had been. "I was proud she took such command of the room."

I knew from this experience that Erika was strong. I also sensed she was going to make it emotionally. Erika's resilience would carry her through the challenges life threw her way.

As the school was kind enough to give Erika a full scholarship, I volunteered for school activities, such as the annual auction and cooking for the teacher lunches. But as I sat at that first meeting studying with younger women, I thought, *this shouldn't be my role at age sixty.* I felt lost as the women spoke about scouting venues. My mind wandered back to a couple of years earlier when visiting Charla. Late at night, I walked downstairs to get a glass of water. She'd fallen asleep on the floor with her clothes on next to a snoring Sparkles. Charla slept a foot away from the kitchen door. She would go, and go until she dropped.

The next day she laughed and said she didn't realize petting Sparkles would lull her to sleep. "I'm exhausted from the auction."

Erika started soccer practice two days a week after school and on Saturdays. My work schedule remained flexible, and I was able to be there for every practice. I tried my best to be enthusiastic at her games, but she never paid attention to me. I wondered if her other family made derogatory remarks about me or if I was being paranoid. But I did sense Erika was emotionally distant from me.

During Joan's time at the practices, Joan stayed in her car and the two of us remained on opposite sides of the field as we did in court. I could not bring myself to walk over to her car and say hello.

While driving home one evening, Erika said, "Grandma, I want to go back and gain a black belt in Tae Kwon Do, because before my mom died, I'd been working towards that."

She impressed me with how well she explained it. "Of course, honey, we can fit it into our schedule."

I took a deep breath. I had to figure out a way to pay for those classes. *Maybe Joan would contribute...*

Thankfully, Joan said yes. Thus, our new adventure began driving across the city twice a week to Master Wheatly's gym. The gym was closer to Joan's house, and it relieved me that one day was on her schedule. That gave me time to clean our house. Somehow, inside of this crowded routine, I squeezed in Erika taking piano and knitting lessons as well. I was a full-blown, modern mother doing it all, and had the hair-pulling stress to prove it.

Driving Erika home one night after martial arts class, I remembered the custody judge strongly recommended that we attend a grief group affiliated with and paid for by the state. I didn't want to go. It just seemed like too much effort.

I caved in and invited Erika to attend the children's section. A woman escorted her into another building. My heart raced because the building was in a rough part of town, and I felt uneasy watching her walk away. Just a while ago, her other family had hired guards in case of a potential kidnapping. Now, the State allowed strangers to take her into an annexed building in a questionable part of town.

In my room, twenty people filed in, both men and women sat in aluminum chairs. A few stood up and revealed their heart-break. Each story was as tragic as the one before. "After I had two bouts of cancer, my child died in a drowning accident."

"A car crash killed my husband and son."

Right away, I realized the group leader would only interject for break time, but never offer guidance. He was just a body in the room. Devoid of hope and inspiration, I felt more depressed than when I arrived.

For several weeks, the same people stood and portrayed the same stories. A couple of new people threaded through with their tragic tales. Each terrible time, I repeated my story. At the end of the meeting, it felt like the room was covered with lead. I desperately desired an encouraging, inspiring facilitator. Tony Robbins anyone?

That first night I had asked Erika afterward as we got into the car, "How was it for you?"

She shrugged. "It was fine."

After our third visit, we had just left the place. I insisted. "Erika, for real, what's it like in your group?"

"Well, the same kids share the same awful stories."

I stopped, turned, and faced her. "I don't want to come anymore. But I'll bring you and just do some shopping to pass the time—what do you think?"

"Grandma, I'd rather not come either—it's too yucky. It makes me feel yuckier. I want to be happy."

We didn't look at each other, but I smiled and believed she did too. I said, "I didn't like it right away, but assumed you needed it."

"I thought *you* liked it, so I didn't say anything either." It was the first time we finally clicked on something.

Even though we agreed on the misery of the meetings, Erika and I continued a strained relationship in that she kept quiet and I withheld most of the time as well. I hoped that if I made her nourishing food, drove her to her lessons, went to her events, watched shows with her, and read stories to her, that eventually we would find enough harmony, she would see my love.

Overall, I felt nervous around her as I couldn't ground into my loving footing as I had with my two children. Lost, I stayed tangled inside myself ...

Later, I smiled at the irony that group therapy had ultimately worked for us, just not in the way the State intended. It had brought Erika and me closer, and I'd shown good faith, which was crucial in family court.

The judge had also suggested Erika get private professional counseling. I contacted Dr. Joann Lippert, who was recommended to me. During the first session, I stayed and observed. Dr. Lippert had Erika play with certain toys and games while she remained silent in a chair, observing. Dr. Lippert never moved from her seat or said anything. I knew Erika enough to sense boredom. The session left me uninspired.

Despite my discontent with Dr. Lippert, I arranged for Joan and I to schedule a joint counseling session with her. Too stressed to seek someone new, I gave the doctor a pass—trusting she might use a different approach with adults.

There was only a small couch in the room, thus Joan and I sat close together–too close. I started first by mentioning that Erika enjoyed soccer and Tae Kwon Do. Joan's face lit up. "When Darren was a teen, he loved baseball, and he'd been a star player in high school and was even scouted to play in the big leagues. But then he got hurt, and all of that fell away. It was unfortunate his injuries were too extensive for him to continue."

It astounded me how dismissive Joan's behavior was around me. She'd already told this story at Erika's soccer practice in front of several mothers as I stood there. Now here it was

again. I just kept reflecting on our holidays and dinners together. All those years when she was consistently an hour late when I massaged her and I was so patient with her. I had done everything I could to make her feel uplifted by being of service. *Can she not see how hard it is for me to hear this?* I changed the conversation. “By the way, Joan, how many times are you taking Erika to see Darren?”

“As much as I can.”

Joan stared straight ahead. I could hardly contain myself. I imagined being a female wrestler throwing her on the ground. I waited for Dr. Lippert to say something—anything like, “Well Joan, can you see from Soorya’s perspective that what you just said might be bothersome?” Nothing.

Instead, the doctor merely wrote in a notebook–the same as when she and Erika were together. Disappointed with both women for different reasons, I balanced myself, by imagining smoke secreting out of my ears.

Apprehensive that Dr. Lippert would write a negative report on me, I remained silent. From everything I’d experienced and read, family court is completely subjective, based on whether the judge likes you or not. I simply could not get a negative report. I wasn’t sure what that would have meant but I wasn’t taking any chances.

At Erika’s second session with Dr. Lippert, I left her alone. Afterward, I asked her the same question as before. “How did it go?”

“It’s boring because the doctor never talks to me. I hate it like that other place.”

I called and canceled her next appointment the following morning. Erika’s evaluation was spot on.

I searched for another therapist for Erika. This is when I found Dori Orlich. Dori was a dream, and I knew Erika liked her. Unfortunately, Erika said, "You and Dori are friends, so I can't tell her what's really bothering me about you."

No matter how much I struggled to convince Erika that Dori was a professional and that she would never divulge information, Erika shook her head and only went to her a few times. From that point on, Erika never received another therapy session with anyone. I worried about that but had faith that she would find her way. I would not force her—I thought that might ultimately be more damaging.

Chapter 21
Foster Kittens

I enjoyed washing dishes in the open kitchen connected to our living room. It was easy to observe Erika knitting on the couch in front of me as she watched children's shows. I relaxed more with our relationship because she seemed content. Sometimes she would hum or talk to herself while stitching her pattern. Erika started a business knitting for friends. She called her work "Planet Yarn."

One day as I darted to take something out of the oven, Erika appeared, grinning, as she tugged on my apron. "What?"

"Grandma, can we ple-e-e-ase get a puppy?"

"No. I can't deal with that, plus keeping up my busy schedule. I'm sorry because I hate refusing you, but I just can't do it."

"Well ... can we at least care for kittens then?"

I groaned inwardly because "taking care" of kittens was still a lot of work—for me.

"What's your idea?"

"When I volunteered a couple of weeks ago, I saw a litter, and it would be fun to take them all in, plus the momma cat."

"Ok, I guess we can try it," I said, having to sprout the seeds in my brain.

I knew I was in trouble once Erika's class visited the Humane Society. The staff gifted her a T-shirt and declared her a "Professional Petter." Erika had not stopped talking about the animals since.

My concern was for Tara, my cat I'd inherited back from Charla. Tara had already been through a lot, and she was territorial, more like a feral cat. And mamma cats are fiercely protective. I imagined them fighting. I didn't know how adding in feisty kittens would work either.

That night, I took a bath, thinking it was my last relaxing moment of freedom before kitten care. This added responsibility was surely also predictable heartache, but I couldn't say no to Erika's wishes.

I'd seen animal provisions stuffed in one of Charla's boxes in the garage. Dog leashes and dozens of cat toys were stuffed inside a couple of carrying cases. I chose the medium crate and placed a pillow inside to make it comfy for kitties.

At the Washoe County Humane Society, the staff informed us we had to register as foster care providers. I liked how they asked meticulous, candid questions about our lives, such as how loyal we felt to the animal we were adopting. Another was would we endure an animal even if it became annoying?

Once we finished the paperwork, I thought of dashing to my car and backing out, because of the sadness of letting go of them. Worst of all, I foresaw still worrying about the Humane Society finding homes for the mothers, since they were not in the kitten category.

Erika already had her hand inside a cage petting something. "Grandma, these are the ones." A mama cat with brown and yellow patches barely looked up at us as she licked one of her babies.

The first litter was a breeze. Erika wanted her bedroom of course, and we placed the box full of infants down beside her nightstand on the floor with fluffy bedding.

Mamma slowly relaxed a little more every time I walked near her. Even though taking care of the new additions was as much work as I dreaded, there was also a wholesome satisfaction for both Erika and me. We were bonding in a fresh way.

But there is always a fly in the soup: Tara was predictably unsettled and annoyed. At least she left mamma and the babies alone. Even though I felt unsettled that she was miserable over our guests, Erika's elation overruled my regret for Tara. She spent most of her free time giggling and throwing strings at those feisty babies. Of course, I ended up doing all the cleanup.

Erika and I didn't get too attached to the first litter, and I only cried briefly after returning them.

With our next group, Erika fell in love. She named her favorite, Devon. "Grandma, Devon is different. He's really smart."

Often during the day, she commented on how gifted this little soul was. Devon was a fat, roly-poly, almost Angora fur ball with black spot markings.

By the time Devon's family of five was ready to return to the Humane Society, I had adopted three of them to friends. Torn about whether to keep Devon, I finally said yes at the last minute. Ha! Only one litter in, and we already had a new pet!

I couldn't sleep all night because of the *remaining* boy kitten. By morning, I was an emotional wreck, worse than attending court, and decided if no one had taken him, I would.

Whether fate farted or sprouted, that kitten was in a cuddle ball in his cage the next morning, inside a tiny fleece sleeping bag. His white fur had a bit of gray around his nose. He seemed heavenly. I instantly named him Angel.

Once Angel entered our house, he and Devon tumbled and licked each other. Even though my new chore was to shovel extra cat waste, Erika and I were a more complete family.

Although Erika and I disagreed about the spelling of Devon's name. She insisted on "Devin," but for me, it looked too close to the devil, so I begged for "Devon." And it rhymed with "heaven" (although, when I thought about it, Devin did too.) She refused to budge, so when I wrote about him to friends, I spelled his name my way and when she wrote, she spelled it her way.

We took pictures. Oh boy, did we take pictures. One day, I realized we didn't have a single shot of Erika or me. They were all photos of kittens! Through our continual fostering of litters for a year, Erika and I found a haven to experience laughter. My only regret to this day was not adopting one baby who cuddled, purred in my ear, and expressed love. I'm sure she would have been the *purfect* companion. But then again, I would have become the Cat Lady ...

Chapter 22
Criminal Defense

As I struggled to make a living, cover my bills, and care for Erika, the legal system was still in high gear, and it left my head spinning as civil and criminal cases became intertwined.

The State of Nevada's criminal case against Darren commenced with a motion that stated, "He stabbed her body repeatedly, striking her with a knife or sharp object on her leg, forearm, wrist, and throat. The resulting injuries included the severance of Charla's left carotid artery, her esophagus, and her trachea. He also inflicted injuries that resulted in blunt force trauma to large portions of her body."

After reading the motion, I began having respiratory problems. There was a subtle wheezing as I breathed. I couldn't manage one more problem, so I didn't bother seeing a doctor.

Darren's lawyer, Scott Freeman, moved to claim that the courts should drop the attempted murder charge for using a high-powered rifle on June 12th. Freeman stated in the motion, "It is equally as possible that it came from a weapon discharged by someone other than Darren Mack. We know of at least three other people who are or were royally upset with Judge Weller and his rulings, one of whom allegedly has a 'personality disorder'. To conclude, even as a matter of probability, that Darren Mack attempted to murder Judge Weller is to engage in pure speculation."

The *Reno Gazette-Journa*l reported Freemen was also dismayed that the Justice of the Peace, Dannan, had refused a psychiatrist to evaluate Darren. Since Darren's lawyers were striving to get him off via an insanity plea, they needed a psychiatrist to declare him insane.

Darren's lawyers then filed a motion to remove all Washoe District Court judges from all civil and criminal cases against him because of potential bias. Within ten days, Senior Judge J. Thompson disqualified all Washoe County judges from handling any of the civil cases involving Darren Mack.

Two weeks later, Nevada Supreme Court Chief Justice Robert Rose assigned the six civil cases to two judges from neighboring counties. The higher court appointed Judge Huff of the Third Judicial District for Charla and Darren Mack's divorce case.

In October, Egan moved to freeze Darren's pension plan of $750,000 to preserve those resources for Erika, enabling me to use a portion to raise her and pay for mounting legal fees. Darren's civil attorney, Mark Wray, argued the pension monies were not part of Charla's estate; a judge froze the account for thirty days, allowing both sides to file motions that a federal court would hear next.

It felt like lawsuits flew around me like kites. Judge Weller went back to work and his assistant, Annie Allison, filed a civil lawsuit against Darren. She asked for $50,000 because she'd "suffered extreme shock, horror, terror, and fear for my life." I was also astounded to read that a lingering ten-year probate case involving Darren's first wife Debra, came forth to settle as well.

Also coming to court was Joan Mack's civil suit against Charla for not returning her diamond ring and Rolex watch, both gifts from Darren, to the Palace Jewelry store, where Darren had obtained them.

Mark Wray, Darren's civil attorney, was satisfied that all the civil cases would now move forward outside of Washoe County. Freeman and Chesnoff had success in bringing Judge Herndon from Las Vegas, and Special Prosecutor Christopher Lalli came in from Las Vegas for Darren's case. So even though I didn't hire a lawyer from Las Vegas, Las Vegas energy came to Reno.

Three weeks later, Prosecutor Lalli moved that Darren Mack was fully competent to stand trial.

I read all the names in the newspaper and wondered what these cases cost. I received no child support as the Macks still fought that.

All I wanted to do was cook, make a home for Erika, and play with our felines. Instead of lawsuits, what I cared about were paw disputes. My social network centered on how Tara tolerated Angel and Devon (Devin). To make things worse, I had given away their brother Rudi, to a woman who suddenly died. Poor Rudi stayed in her apartment alone for two weeks before someone helped him. They brought him over one night in a large box. Out popped a gigantic black and white cat, and there he was. Surprise! So now we had four cats, and of course, all the foster meows. And of course, Tara. Within a second, I fell madly in love with jock-like, stocky Rudi. So instantly, and though I'd resisted it, I became the Cat Lady.

A major situation broke out, and it wasn't in the press. Devon forgot he was the brother of Rudi and became wildly jealous. He sprayed urine everywhere to let us know. Through some kind of miraculous providence, I now bartered with a South African guy, Pierre, who owned a carpet cleaning business. Pierre was such a character—he continued to call me "Young Lady" no matter how many times I asked him not to. Pierre loved our massage trades so much that he would zip over and steam-clean on my whim, and because of Devon using his urine as a weapon, it was sometimes twice a week.

The dramatic climax unleashed when Devon hopped on a sleeping Erika in bed, squatted and peed on her face. She was hysterical. Being the clever fixer of problems, I quickly got out aromatherapy oil of pure, extracted roses, and placed a dot on each cat's nose. I left the room and came back within a minute. To my joy and speechless surprise, Rudi and Devon were chest-to-chest smashed together, licking each other's faces. From that point on, Devon never squirted on Erika or the furniture again.

Chapter 23
Wrongful Death and Diet

The human adventures continued. Egan and Attorney Kent Robinson teamed up and pursued a wrongful death suit for the Charla Mack estate. Both lawyers assured me they would not charge me for their efforts. "We want to bring this forward on behalf of Erika," Egan said.

"This has nothing to do with the state's prosecution?" I asked.

"No, this is a separate issue. We are suing Darren for taking Erika's mother away, and he should reimburse her for that."

I felt honored that these men provided this gift for her. They didn't seek a specified amount in the suit, which they referred to as "compensatory, special, general, and punitive damages."

The appointed administrator, Randy Kuckenmeister, filed the suit. Randy had been Charla's friend and helped her with her divorce case, keeping her financial records straight. Charla had loved Randy. It comforted me that he was on board.

The suit stated, "During the marriage, Darren Mack was physically abusive of Charla Mack, causing significant and substantial emotional and physical pain and suffering. Before Charla Mack died, she unsuccessfully attempted to defend herself, sustaining additional wounds and injuries in her effort to defend herself. From the initiation of Defendant Mack's attack on Charla Mack to the time of her death, [she] experienced sustained severe physical and emotional pain, disfigurement, and anguish.

"Given the sufficient financial condition of Darren Mack and in light of the malicious, vicious, willful, and deliberate nature of his fatal attack on Charla Mack, punitive damages should be awarded in the maximum amount allowed by law."

To get ready for this trial, these kind lawyers asked for a photo of Erika that they could show the jurors. I chose a large framed one that a professional photographer had taken. Erika wore a pink fairy dress, and she lingered in a meadow looking into a pond. The setting was magical, with pink and blue hues. It was an unusual shot because Erika's head turned downward as her face reflected in the water.

I was grateful I had nothing to do with this lawsuit except show up in court. I didn't have to testify. The jury was made up of eighteen women and men. No one from the Mack family attended. It seemed everyone was on our side.

Both Egan Walker and Kent Robinson thoroughly explained to the jury how brutally Darren murdered Charla. What hit me hardest with what these two lawyers said was about Darren leaving Erika to deal with all the scattered fragments of her life and how she would continue to face the betrayal of her father, who remained alive. The jury came back a few hours later with a verdict. Erika would receive the Palace Jewelry store after Joan's death. They also awarded her five hundred million dollars, the largest award of its kind in the history of the State of Nevada for a wrongful death lawsuit. In the end, we didn't see a penny as a result of this decision.

Egan stopped and turned to look at me when we got to our cars. "It's just funny money because no one will ever pay that. The Macks don't have this kind of cash, but the jury wanted the world to know how they felt about this heinous crime. But for sure, Erika will receive all the funds from Darren's estate, and she will get the pawnshop."

"She is too young, and I worry others will raid the valuables in Joan's basement before she can get to it."

"Well, Erika is a smart girl, and I'm betting it's all going to turn out for her."

I knew Erika would share with her brother and sister equally, and on that level, the suit had been unnecessary, but hidden factors could erupt in the future, so I trusted the results of that lawsuit might come in handy one day if needed.

My beloved cat Tara disappeared immediately after the wrongful death suit, which filled me with added grief. The last time I'd looked at her, she'd taken my breath away with her silky black fur and brilliant emerald eyes staring up at me. I had lost another incredible, unique being.

As I mourned Tara, Kristin Monibe, Erika's new caseworker from Social Services called. "Soorya, Joan has brought it to our attention that since you are a vegan, Erika might not be getting proper nutrition in her diet."

"Wait … Joan knew Charla was a vegetarian her entire life. Joan asked me for nutritional advice for her diabetes and I gave it to her … This is phony. She just wants to break me financially."

One can go through a negative experience and endure it. Then there are experiences where having what you stand for questioned makes you want to go berserk. Every nerve in your body is ready to fight. My emotions that day fell into the latter category.

"Soorya, would you be willing to write everything you feed Erika in a two-week period? Your efforts would help us assess Joan's consideration."

"Sure, no problem."

Joan's latest aggression so irritated me that I jumped in my car and went to the gym to exercise before I lost my temper and called her.

After working out, I decided not to confront her in any way.

Instead, I painstakingly wrote down every food I prepared for Erika. I even measured the protein contents along with the fat and sugar ratios.

I sent to Kristin:

Breakfast: Oatmeal, and freshly squeezed organic vegetable juices made from celery, kale, carrots, cucumber, parsley, (and slices of apple to cut the bitter kale).

Charla was nervous about Erika getting adequate vitamin B12, as a veggie, so I honor my daughter by keeping eggs in her diet whenever Erika wants them with sourdough or seed toast.

Lunch & Dinner: Montessori has an organic garden where the children work, and once a week the students pick the vegetables and make salads together. The other four days, I make beans, nuts, and seed patties, and of course, food that children prefer, like spaghetti, veggie hot dogs, or grilled vegan cheese sandwiches.

Dessert: I push frozen bananas and berries through a juicer to make 'ice cream', and I make homemade chocolate sauce from Cacao with nuts and blueberries on top. Erika also gets snacks from the health food store.

No one called back regarding my food list, so I assumed all went well.

Joan's custody time, on the other hand, was always stressful for me. One day, I drove over to pick Erika up and Joan opened the door. "We got home late and Erika hasn't eaten. Be right with you."

I placed my purse down on the table and watched Joan microwave Erika a can of soup. I had to laugh after I shook my head. *She is such a piece of work.*

Chapter 24
Mediation and a Lesson

Has anyone heard a rooster at dawn? You know it's a damn rooster—correct? Have you ever wondered if the distant car was a police car? Then once one is directly behind, you understand without a doubt. This is how convinced I was that Darren fed his mother winstructions to remove me from having anything to do with Erika.

The latest affidavit Egan received stated that Joan would not agree for me to gain child support, and she would see me in court. Joan, who I always thought was her own person, once again baffled me. I wondered why she wasn't pondering the core character of her son, instead. Without a doubt, she wanted to satisfy him.

Later I found out from Egan that Darren fought from his cell, preventing the release of the funds Judge Weller had awarded Charla right before her death, which came from their trust. Joan had turned into Darren's tool. This father wasn't interested in the welfare of his "angel." He just wanted me gone.

The ironic and weird fact was that I was still managing shock, and had no clue that Egan worked to transfer a portion of the cash awarded to Charla to me via child support. I thought the State of Nevada would pay through some kind of fund, and the Macks protested *that.* It's challenging to imagine how naïve and misinformed I was. Shock is a complex thing and Egan assumed the logic—that I understood what he pursued. I didn't.

From Darren's point of view, he shot Judge Weller over granting Charla one-ninth of their savings. He murdered his wife over receiving it. Now, a portion of that cash might flow to me, which enraged him. Basically, that meant he murdered her for nothing.

The same day Egan called about the latest affidavit, I discovered I had also blown through my meager savings. Even though a mysterious donor was sending me $200 monthly through a bank account with no name on it, I still couldn't pay all the bills. (later, I found out that the mysterious donor was another angel, Chandra Mayer.)

I charged gas on credit, and found a piggy bank in one of Charla's boxes that contained $175. On certain mornings, Whole Foods Market grocers peeled off bruised parts of the vegetables and threw the top layers into the trash. The trash, being a large can lined with a fresh hefty bag—was clean and the grocer even wore rubber gloves. As I picked through the discarded vegetables—underneath, they looked fine, except for a few brown spots, which I could easily remove. Plus, being in a health food store, most of the vegetables were organic. I asked the grocer if he minded if I took them for my "chickens"? The young guy said, "Sure, no problem."

I made fast friends with that grocer, and every time I needed to, I routinely gathered vegetables out of the bin. They worked great for casseroles, soups, and sautéed veggies. I felt proud of being resourceful.

My scavenger efforts brought no embarrassment, but time had run out—I had to find another job. Within a few days, I interviewed at the Utopia Day Spa. It was all the way across the city near where Joan lived. This was a gas disadvantage, but the owner was a kind lady, and since she watched my story unravel in the news, she understood I'd have to take time off for the trials. "I'm willing to accommodate you, Soorya," she said, and then hugged me.

The blessings kept coming, as I could maneuver around Erika's schedule, taking her to soccer practice and her lessons. I just had to coordinate about booking my sessions.

All the therapists at Utopia were kind. I'd never worked in a spa before and I was starting rock bottom building a new clientele. The long-labored hours of back-to-back sessions were hard. My hands throbbed so severely that, at home in the evenings, it forced me to soak them in bowls of ice water for relief. Even though my new job took hard work, I was overjoyed to experience such sweet women. Some days, as I walked by them, I would lightly sing, "This is a love festival," and they always laughed. We women knew we had something rare, as there was no gossip or conflict between us. There was only kindness.

One day I mentioned to my other therapists that I would drive to Los Angeles to take Erika to Los Angeles for Christmas with Jamie and Allie, Erika's friends. A facial therapist secretly started a collection for me to have extra cash so I could treat Erika to Disneyland while there. She placed a check inside a lovely card and all the therapists signed it. They surprised and deeply touched me. For all the awful occurrences of having to go to court and face the daily articles about Darren in the newspaper, Utopia was just that.

I often had to speed to my first job, Steamboat Hot Springs, in between sessions at Utopia. It was intense driving back and forth, then having to get Erika from the Montessori pickup line. Even though there was less personal time, I could, thankfully, manage the bills better. For the expenses that I still couldn't handle, like Erika's orthodontist and dentist, I made payments as I did on our gasoline bill. Since my son, Christopher, was an adult, and Charla had been on her own for two decades, I'd forgotten how much it cost to raise a child. What hurt me, though, was one day Joan came to my dentist's office to pick Erika up after her treatment for an outing. She said, "Oh, I already had Erika's teeth cleaned two weeks ago."

I panted from lack of oxygen. "Joan! Why didn't you *tell* me? I could have saved money!" More, much more—I was irritated that Erika had to have two sets of toxic X-rays. "I don't understand why you don't partner with me over our granddaughter?"

I spoke loud enough for other patients to hear. Of course, Joan said nothing and went back to reading her magazine while waiting for Erika. I wondered why Erika had said nothing either … I hoped she didn't feel so dominated by me she turned passive again. When I asked her once she came back home, she said, "I don't know, grandma, I didn't think of it." I surmised that she was just a kid with enormous emotional challenges to deal with, and it had nothing to do with me.

While I still fumed over Joan's dental mischief, Social Services called and asked me to write a letter and make it as long or as short as I needed on my opinions, experiences, and feelings concerning Joan Mack. This request was for their assessments to go before the judge to determine permanent custody of Erika. Writing about Joan and my relationship was stressful because I wanted to share how we'd been family, but since the murder, she had been terrible and had backed me into a corner. I needed to reveal deeper insights, and those insights said I didn't think it was appropriate that she raise Erika.

I wrote all of my misgivings and emailed them to Social Services. I declared that Joan's attitude and deceptions, mixed with stories of blind admiration for Darren, could ultimately harm Erika's emotional wellbeing.

Later that afternoon at a soccer practice, Joan walked up to the circle of mothers I engaged with and offered the same comments she had shared when we were in therapy. Joan's voice lilted in cheerfulness. "Darren was so terrific at baseball …"

I tuned her out, thinking about what I would eat that night.

In the distance, her tone caught my attention. "But then he got an injury, and it devastated him. Our family felt bad for him because he could no longer play after that."

No one commented, and each woman left the circle.

I wondered if Joan viewed herself wearing the stigma of shame on her forehead or if she had done enough in the Reno community financially, that she saw herself above us all. For decades, the Mack name held respect for their donations to charities. Influential people in Reno and Las Vegas had admired Dennis Mack before he died. What I knew for sure was that after June 12, 2006, Joan's former standing was gone.

Joan continued to file affidavits for what I considered petty annoyances, things we could have worked out over lunch or simply on a five-minute phone call. When I saw her in person, she was friendly. Then her ugly affidavit would roll in that same week and it felt like she whacked me again. Those filings always meant draining more money and time in court.

In early January, Egan filed a petition asking the judge to enforce payment of the one million dollar divorce settlement meant for Charla before her death. Egan wrote that even though the settlement wasn't signed, it was still valid.

Darren fired his third lawyer, concerning the trust, and now had a new team of civil attorneys. John Springgate and Mark Wray announced themselves as his lawyers. To my astonishment, Mark Wray thought Darren was innocent. Darren had found a fan. Wray requested for the courts to wash their hands and dismiss the entire settlement agreement.

This is how small Reno is: before Darren's appointment of Springgate, I had gone to his wife for treatment after I threw my neck out. She was a highly regarded physical therapist.

I thought it noteworthy that Joan and I would go into a conference room for a final mediation about child support, on April 13, 2007, a Friday. Egan and I drove together that morning. A personalized license plate on a car in front of us said: No Ego.

"Egan look!"

He laughed. "That's interesting; I'll take note."

I added, "I think it's meaningful for me to stay humble and in my truth, no matter what."

Egan placed a thumbs up. "It's always good to stay humble and in one's truth."

Our mediators instructed Joan and me to discuss a contract drafted by Egan and Kevin Ryan, entitled, "Stipulation and Placement Order 432B."

The room, held in the law library, had many police again and other people I didn't know. Darren's son Jory and brother

Lanny attended. Charla's friend and accountant Randy Kuckenmeister was there to advise on financial matters. The Social Services representative for Erika, Kristen Monibi, also attended along with Erika's lawyer and guardian ad litem, Karen Sabo, whom I had become friends with. I'd been communicating with both women for months now and they couldn't have been kinder.

This was the first time I was in the same room as Darren since he murdered my daughter. He sat facing me in chains, wearing an orange prison suit. His clasped fingers disturbed me. I kept thinking of how violent those hands had been, how those hands had brutally butchered my daughter. Hair was cut unevenly, his face never met mine.

Darren spoke first. "No matter what, I don't think Soorya should have the slightest financial support or have custody of my daughter."

I imagined my insides containing cysts that could burst at any moment if I got mad enough. Joan sat all the way across the long room, away from me.

This mediation continued for two agonizing days. Our arbitrator, Cindi-Elaine Heron, kept us on track. Finally, on day two, it was my turn to talk. I addressed the Macks: "All of you were my family before this happened. Joan, I honestly never thought a negative thing about you in the ten years we spent together. We always had uplifting conversations. We used to confide in each other. I loved all of you, and you know what—I still love you, Joan."

I looked at Jory. "I'll always love *you,* Jory. I turned my head. I love you, Lanny."

I swallowed hard and looked at Darren ... my voice was wobbly. "I still love you too, despite everything." I couldn't say his name.

I stared into Darren's eyes, but he kept his gaze distant. A thought flashed through my mind. Toward the end of her marriage, Charla had admitted to me, "Darren doesn't respect you." It shocked me to hear that. I had served him in every way I could. I thought at the time maybe he didn't respect me because I wasn't wealthy. I assumed after helping take care of him when he was sick, we were close. He had bragged to others that he was "The Poster Child in the world for complete recovery of Spinal Meningitis," and a lot of that was from my help. He thanked me daily. It was the only time I received praise from Darren Mack.. Two years before he killed Charla, he had met a multimillionaire whom he bragged about and patterned his life after. The man was a Christian and Darren started going to his church. Charla had rolled her eyes saying he was being fake.

Now, looking at Darren, after all the hell he'd caused, somehow, a calm control took over me. I knew if I couldn't reach Darren's soul, maybe I could at least reach Joan's. I wasn't nervous. The right choice of words came forth. I spoke to her. "When all of this trauma first happened, I came to you outside the police station working on your shoulders, do you remember? I thought we would be two grieving grandmothers building a life together for Erika. But it has been quite the opposite."

Joan said, "I'm not the type to argue or fight."

"You are passive-aggressive. You have wonderful social graces in public, but you behave differently behind the scenes. You also show your aggression through money. Joan, this leads me to ask ... Who. Are. You?" I said those words slowly, deliberately, as I placed my erect hand under my chin and stared into her eyes.

The room went silent. But this moment's pause didn't feel awkward. It was a historical event for me to speak out as the mother of my daughter and also as a human being taking my power.

Our mediator called for a break. I left to grab my notebook from the car. On the way out, I jokingly said to a woman police officer in the hallway, "Finally, I want to kill Darren for his comments." I genuinely thought my dark humor was funny, like when I bantered with Chris or Geni, blowing off steam.

As I walked back into the foyer, two officers blocked my entrance. The officer I'd spoken to apologized. "I felt a need to report what you said. I must frisk you in the bathroom because you might be a danger to our suspect, Mr. Mack.".

I threw my head back and laughed nervously. "I'm in trouble?" My voice was so squeaky and high-pitched it embarrassed me more than my comment.

Two other officers stood by—*just in case … Geez*. The same officer said, "It's standard procedure once someone makes a threatening remark. Please come with me."

The officer guided me against the wall in the lavatory. "I feel bad having to do this," she said as she moved her hands up and down my body. I looked at her badge.

"Officer Jan, I would never, ever, under any circumstance, attempt to kill Mr. Mack. If guards placed me with him alone in a room and I had all the weapons in the world at my disposal, I wouldn't touch a hair on his head." I continued, "I want Mother Nature and karma to take its course with him because then I'll know he'll have a more profound punishment, and I'll have the best justice. Plus, I want him to *live* and think about what he did, and rot in prison. I am the most trustworthy person in the room to leave with Darren. I want him to pay fully and completely for his actions."

Officer Jan faced me with both eyes. "I understand. We have to make sure. It's our job. Have a nice day."

Officer Jan and I walked out of the bathroom together, and I went back into court. The experience had shaken me, though. I realized Friday the 13th had indeed been about "no ego," and that included my smugness of joking that I would kill Darren to a police officer. I remembered something I had dreamed of once. A voice had spoken to me: "To be a saint, one must find neutrality in all things."

The police escorted Darren to the Sparks jail by two pm on the second day. Egan leaned over and whispered to me in court, "They're getting him out of here because it was obvious he enjoys fighting and staying out of jail."

For the next two hours, Joan and I debated. Three minutes before shutdown at five pm, like a miracle, Joan relented and signed an agreement stating that I would receive child support. To this day, I still find it challenging to believe how naïve I was, though, having no clue we were negotiating for the extraction of money out of Darren's pension, which would become Erika's trust.

Chapter 25
A Trial in Las Vegas

September 2007

Darren's criminal trial for the murder of my daughter was now in full swing. My mind went back to a call I received in 2005 from Charla when she interrupted my warm greeting.

"Darren just choked me!"

"Oh my God—what happened?"

"We were outside in the parking lot at Jory's dentist. We argued while Jory got in the car. He slammed his car door in my face. I actually had to jump back for the door not to hit me. I got mad and threw some pebbles at his bumper. He screeched to a halt, jumped out, threw me onto the pavement, and choked me—hard! I thought he was going to kill me right there in the parking lot."

"Did you call the police?"

"No, because I don't want him to lose his pawn license. Then he won't be able to support the family. It would screw up his work. I don't want him to have a record."

"Charla, he could have killed you … damaged your vocal cords."

"He choked me once before, but I didn't tell anyone. Lisa called him a few minutes ago and said "You'd better keep your hands in your pants if you don't want the police arresting you." Charla's voice cracked, and then she sobbed harder.

"Charla, listen to me. You've got to *stop* challenging him. Take whatever deal he gives you and get out!"

"I know. He damaged my throat; I can barely swallow."

"I'm going to call him! I've been keeping my distance so he'll give me Erika on his time. If I alienate him, he'll always say no, but I'm talking to that bastard."

"No, you are right to stay clear. I think Lisa said enough for him to stop."

"I'm so sorry, my darling daughter."

"I know. I love you."

Two days later Darren contacted Charla by email and said they'd run out of money, that there was nothing left in their checking accounts. During that ordeal, I had to force myself not to dwell on how much Charla was suffering … Lisa had advised her to take out a credit card, because she said Darren's next move would be to hurt her financially. As predicted her card failed, so she whipped out the new one at the check stand with a load of groceries the week of Christmas. She didn't miss a beat for her survival.

Judge Herndon and lawyers for both sides met to work through any last-minute difficulties before jury selection. National media arrived in Reno, and film crews set up outside, around the courthouse, filling the block. *What if Darren got off like OJ?*

Christopher couldn't fly west for this part of the trial, but Chandra and Ann Mudd came for support. Judge Douglas Herndon, entered the courtroom at 10 am and apologized for wearing jeans under his blue robe. "The airline has lost my luggage. I'm not trying to set a new fashion for judges." Laughter lightened the tense courtroom.

Out of the five hundred potential jurors who received questionnaires, two hundred and fifty responded that Darren: Dingle Berry was guilty. Judge Herndon thought that there was still hope for a fair trial with the remaining jurors.

I kept squirming in my seat because the microphones were poor and I couldn't hear much. By 5:00 pm, I realized the lawyers had only approved three men and three women.

Darren's lawyer, David Chesnoff moved for a change of venue because he said several of the potential jurors had been "less than candid," desiring to be part of a famous trial.

Early the next morning, and before all of us sat down, Judge Herndon announced he was moving the trial to Clark County, Las Vegas. *Oh no. I wonder how I will take care of Erika.* My thoughts churned, worrying about how to piece together my fragmented life.

Judge Herndon asked Darren, "Do you agree with the change?"

"Very much so, sir," Darren replied. His voice carried his course leader rich overtones.

"This case caused me to lose a lot of sleep over the past few nights," the judge said, sighing. Around age fifty, Judge Herndon had beautiful silky skin and looked in shape. Chandra whispered to me, "Your Honor is cute."

The new Las Vegas trial date was set for October 15. The estimated cost was over $100,000 since witnesses now had to be flown in, along with family staying in hotels. I felt gratitude to the taxpayers since I didn't have to pay for my flight or room.

To get away from the chaos, I took a hike near a wilderness area a few minutes from our house. At the top of the hill, I spread out a towel and lay down. No one was around and the fresh air rejuvenated me. *Charla, if only you could come into my body and change places. You'd love all this court drama.*

Charla had been a sleuth whiz. That part of her was what infuriated Darren because she was always two steps ahead of him. I wished I had recorded her stories: "And then he met this woman at the bar when he said he was out with guy friends. I hid several tables over and watched them. He never suspected." Charla's laughter bordered on a witch's cackle when she thought she was clever. I knew underneath, though, that she suffered and cried by how poorly Darren was treating her.

After I arrived home, parents from Erika's school, Denise and Rick Reighly, whose daughter was friends with Erika, called. "Hey, I heard on the news that the trial moved to Vegas. Do you want me to keep Erika while you are there?"

"Yes! Your offer is a godsend as it allows me to be present at the trial. This is the perfect solution!"

Denise and Rick were some of the most caring parents I'd met at Montessori. Rick often dropped everything to come over and help me with minor carpentry jobs whenever I called. Denise had taken one of our sick kittens overnight and, when he was on the brink of death, saved his life using her remedies. Thankfully, and since Joan would be in court as well, they were solving my problem of where Erika could stay.

Detectives flew Darren to Las Vegas on October 9. Prison authorities sent him to a cell module, which held thirty-three inmates. Later an inmate would reveal through the detective grapevine that he was "touched by how wonderful Darren Mack was and so sensitive to his situation."

Darren was such a masterful manipulator that he even could charm hardened criminals.

Chandra and I flew into the Vegas airport and met Charla's best friend Lisa. We stayed at a hotel a block from the courthouse.

The following morning, at 9:30, Ann, Chandra, and I passed what seemed like dozens of media trucks walking into the Clark County Courthouse. This time, along with the regular press, a local station and Court TV filmed. The entire building was much larger than Reno's and had more human activity.

Once seated, I saw my former husband, Jan, in the room. "Are you ready for nutty?" I asked, crossing my eyes and sticking my tongue out, attempting to lighten the heaviness.

Jan rolled his eyes. "I think so. You are right—this is beyond nutty."

"Right? This is beyond the beyond."

Jan shook his head. "Darren."

Nothing more to say as he said it all. Jan and I had married in our early twenties, and even though we weren't right for each other, we had remained friends. Of everything I ever imagined Jan and I would endure, the murder of our daughter was not it. Just then, Christopher Lalli approached. "Would you guys come with me down the hall so we can talk? I need to speak to you in private."

We entered a small room with a single table, four folding chairs, and one window. Lalli began, "Robert Daskas and I want to know your opinion on Darren receiving the death penalty. I can push for that if you choose."

I stood up and walked over to the window. There was cement everywhere. From our height, people moved back and forth like ants. Lalli turned his head. "What do you think, Mr. Sampsel?"

"Call me Jan … I'm not sure. Soorya, what do you think?"

"Here's the deal: I don't want the children to suffer anymore, and I think experiencing another death of a second parent would be too traumatizing. Plus, Darren would take as many appeals as possible, which would cost the state a bundle and drag everything out. He'd be in the press for years to come, which would mean our families would be there with him. There would be no peace for our children at their schools. Families would gossip. My answer is *no*. One more thing—and this is important: As I told a policewoman recently, I want that sucker to suffer. By dying, he'd be let off the hook."

"I'll go with Soorya."

"Okay, that ties it up. I think we're finished here." Mr. Lalli gathered papers off the desk and stood.

Our meeting took ten minutes … ten minutes to determine the fate of another human being.

Jan left with Mr. Lalli. I walked separately as Darren's brother passed by. A flood of emotion ripped through me. "Lanny, may I speak to you?"

He stopped. "What's up?"

"I just want to say that I think our families still can build that bridge of love for Erika's, Jory's, and Elise's sake. And once you realize all the lies Darren has told you …"

I meant to finish, "I think you'll understand even more," but Lanny gritted his teeth and lashed out before stomping away. "Don't you dare talk to me again!"

Oops. I regretted adding the 'lies' part, because that set Lanny off, thinking I was manipulating him. My words stumbled against his stiff posture. A police officer approached. "Ma'am, Mr. Mack said you harassed him. Don't talk to him again during this trial, or there could be consequences."

"Okay, Officer. My bad."

I had wanted to express hope for our families to get along. Yet, since the disaster, every encounter I had with Joan and Lanny always turned sour.

Contrasting the Reno struggle, jury selection in Las Vegas had gone smoothly the day before; the desired selection that Judge Herndon requested occurred right away. Stark difference: Las Vegas citizens didn't know who Darren Mack was yet.

When I walked back into the courtroom after meeting with Christopher Lalli, Darren was positioned in front, on the defendant's side of the courtroom. He wore a tailored black suit, tie, and white shirt. Joan and Alecia Biddison sat in a row behind him. All twelve jurors were seated as well. None looked my way.

KLAS-TV Web TV broadcast the trial live as prosecutor Robert Daskas spoke first. Daska questioned Dan Osborn, Darren's high school friend, who had been at Darren's condo on the morning of the murder was there. Darren had written Dan's name first on his to-do list for him to take Erika to Joan's house before he began the destruction. Dan explained the details of how he and Erika heard his dog barking frantically.

After leaving the stand, I left the courtroom and quickly joined him in the hall. The reporter/media side of me couldn't help herself. "Dan, do you feel enraged by how Darren deceived and used you as if your life didn't matter?"

I had to walk fast to keep up with him. "Yes," he said, almost whispering, and then disappearing around a corner.

Special Prosecutor Lalli explained how Judge Weller had ordered Darren to pay a specific amount of money in child and spousal support to Charla. Darren paid a pittance, then turned off her utilities instead, declaring he couldn't afford them. Judge Weller had been so upset he threatened to throw Darren in jail. *God, if only the judge had done that!* Instead, he merely placed a financial restraining order on their accounts and forbade both to dispose of or hide assets.

Right after Judge Weller's decision, Darren transferred his voting interest in the Palace Jewelry store to his mother, Joan Mack, and filed for bankruptcy. While Darren claimed he was poor, Charla discovered that he regularly paid thousands of dollars to take women he met on online dating sites to fly them across the country and put them in luxurious resorts where he would meet them.

As recounted by the State prosecutor, Charla's lawyer, Shawn Meador, asked Judge Weller to hold Darren in contempt for violating the order. Once again, Judge Weller only gave Darren harsh words, which bitterly disappointed Charla. It was a tragic irony that we all felt the judge went easy on Darren, while Darren claimed Judge Weller was unfair and cruel to him, and therefore tried to kill him to take revenge.

What might have saved my daughter's life was that when Darren's attorney offered Charla close to a million dollars in the original divorce settlement, she agreed and took the deal. But at the last minute, Darren reneged.

Special Prosecutor Lalli addressed the jury. "Darren had seller's remorse. He filed pleadings with the family court, asking for permission to back out of the deal he proposed. The defendant met up with several men from fathers' rights groups, advocates who thought certain judges were biased against fathers. Their mission, their goal, was to change family court for fathers. They thought it unconstitutional, and that there should be a revolt to fix the problem."

Darren's emotional issues didn't find a remedy by attending the father's liberation meetings. His online media aggression increased with outrage, claiming Judge Weller was destroying his life and that he had to "stand up for America" and do something radical to change a hideously corrupt system.

Special Prosecutor Lalli played a tape of Darren being interviewed on a television program called *On Second Thought*. Darren alleged the entire judicial system was corrupt.

All Darren's antics didn't make a difference because Judge Weller would not allow Darren to renege on his financial offer, which inflamed him further.

"The defendant's frustration and anger grew," Lalli said. "The agreement he had proposed months earlier—the one he had tried so hard to back out of—was indeed enforceable. Darren Mack had a problem. Eighteen days later, he found a solution. Darren Mack ambushed his soon-to-be ex with a knife. Her death was neither sudden nor painless. It was personal. She was stabbed multiple times, and even though the defendant was much bigger, Charla Mack didn't go without a fight."

Lalli explained Charla had "classic defensive wounds to her arms, wrists, and legs."

I looked up at the ceiling. When I was in high school, I was so bored I'd count the manufactured holes in each section of the ceiling. All I could see now were Charla's jagged fingernails clawing to save her life.

"At some point, she was on her back trying to kick her husband, who was armed with a knife. Charla Mack didn't stand a chance."

I went back into shock. I could tell because my blanked-out body could barely hear the prosecutor's words.

Lalli showed the jury the worst photo of Charla, lying on the cement floor garage. Darren stared off somewhere while the prosecutor spoke. "The fatal wound was to her neck area. You can see it was delivered with such force, with such power, it left a gaping hole in her neck. In fact, it severed her carotid artery. Charla Mack died on the garage floor of her soon-to-be ex-husband's townhouse while her daughter waited upstairs, watching television."

Explaining how Darren moved further to stalk and shoot Judge Weller, Lalli said, "It was fortuitous that Judge Weller was facing the window sideways and the bullet fragment skipped off his chest. It probably saved his life."

I looked over at Joan Mack. Her head bobbed and her eyes closed. *What a strange time to be drifting off …* My instincts assured me it wasn't strange at all. It was just Joan.

Chapter 26
Problems

Lalli approached the jurors, describing the events as "overwhelming," the Special Prosecutor asserted powerfully that Darren had committed both crimes. Pain seared, shooting up my right leg. Next, the jurors would see in Darren's writing how he outlined his plan for that terrible day. Darren turned his body toward the prosecutor and glared.

When detectives searched Darren's condo, they found a yellow pad of paper with a to-do list written in Darren's handwriting on the kitchen table:

DAN…TAKE ERIKA TO JOAN EQUIP

HELEN…APPT. SHAWN MONDAY SOMETIME BUSHMASTER 223 + CLIP

CHEROKEE…JORY (DM) SIDE WINDOW DOWN BLANK VEST

OTHER COREY DRIVEWAY BLK VEST

GARAGE DOOR OPEN JORY SIDE USAS 12 + CLIPS

END PROBLEM. 45 + CLIPS

PUT LEX IN GARAGE/LOCK HOME 40 CAL + CLIPS

PARKING GARAGE—IF YES 243 + AMMO

ATTORNEY OFFICE 22 RIFLE + AMMO
OBTAIN
FILING BOX

The words 'END PROBLEM' shredded my soul. I remembered Charla on her wedding day when she utterly surrendered to Darren with her head back in a passionate kiss wearing her white wedding dress during their first dance. She hadn't been a problem devoting her life to him and their family or making meals every night for him from scratch.

The prosecution ended its case.

The next morning, Darren's lawyer, Scott Freeman, stood at the podium and faced the six men and six women of the jury.

"During their entire marriage, Darren has been a victim of Charla's violence—beating Darren in Elise's bedroom eight to ten times, body-slamming Darren in their bedroom eight to ten times, slapping him in the face at the airport in front of Jory and Elise. Two broken fingers, one where Darren and Charla were attending their Taekwondo class together. Charla was small, but physically fit and *very* accomplished as a Taekwondo student."

Freeman stated my daughter had "a dark side," she was immoral, used drugs, and that she pushed Darren into sex games, while Darren was an innocent bystander.

"Charla's dysfunctional childhood had left her suffering from a borderline personality disorder. She could be sweet and affectionate one moment and abusive the next. Her mood swings were completely unpredictable. This abuse was fueled by alcohol and self-medication. She liked to use the club drug Ecstasy to enhance her experiences."

Thank God my mother and stepfather weren't listening. Grandpa Tom used to call Charla his "little pokey" even into her teens, and it would have mortified him to hear how Freeman degraded his granddaughter to save her murderer. When her autopsy came back, she had no drugs or alcohol in her system.

Darren had already confessed to his lawyers that he had overloaded on Ecstasy most weekends after he moved out of his and Charla's house. Chandra and I shook our heads because she told me she had caught him in the bathroom pleasuring himself while on the drug and making adoring comments about how handsome he was in the mirror. The idea that Charla pushed all of her excesses onto Darren was preposterous.

Darren had dragged my daughter down into the pit of his degeneracy. Somehow, I knew if I dwelled too long on *that*, I might never come back to mental stability. I remembered Lanny's anger in the hallway, telling an officer I had harassed him.

Freeman continued to bash Charla, saying throughout their marriage she made constant, vile threats to Darren, who had a smug smile while Freeman spoke. Darren's obnoxiously long jaw—now clenched and protruding, made him look even more frightening.

Freeman said that Darren always carried a concealed weapon because of the pawn business. Usually, he wore a 40-caliber pistol in his ankle holster. Then the story around the imaginary gun arose like a setting sun over a dunghill: Freeman claimed that since summer, Darren had worn a 22-caliber Derringer pistol, claiming on the morning of the murder he placed this gun in the back of his shorts. Even though the lie annoyed me, I thought it absurd, visualizing how weird it would be to see a gun sticking out in someone's seersucker shorts at the beach. I knew Darren's style for a decade and I'd never seen him wear a gun in his shorts.

Freeman claimed that Jan's wife, Jackie, who had a psychic step-grandmother Santea, from Puerto Rico, warned Darren that someone would steal from him. An employee shortly after that embezzled $250,000, and Freeman said Darren paid more attention to her warnings.

Darren claimed he visited Santea at Jan's house and asked her if the divorce would go through. Freeman roared loud, bringing in a trance-like voice of Santea's, exclaiming she saw blood everywhere. "You can't turn your back on Charla! She will stab you with a knife!"

Santea loved Charla. In reality, she *had* seen blood on *Darren's hands* and she warned Charla when Darren wasn't around to be careful of *him*.

Freeman's horror-movie script continued: Darren couldn't get a concealed weapons permit until later that day, and because of this tremendous fear of Charla, he didn't feel safe enough with just a knife. He went to his mother's house the morning of the murder, entered a room downstairs which was always locked, and opened a set of heirloom guns, taking one and leaving the other in its case.

"Darren went to Starbucks, had a coffee, and called Charla to make sure she was coming to his house."

Freeman's voice grew smoother. "Charla wanted to discuss settling the divorce. She heard Darren was going to appeal Judge Weller's most recent order to settle, and [she] wanted to discuss a potential settlement, without the lawyers, in light of the potential for this appeal."

Thank goodness Judge Herndon didn't look over at me. I kept tapping my foot, and my face broke into hives.

Freeman continued his defense. "Darren met Charla outside that morning. She asked for her Tupperware containers and gave him a bag to bring them to her. As he handed them over, she started a fight over money. Charla threatened Darren with keeping their daughter from him. He told her that is what his former wife, Debby, threatened with his two other children." Freeman paused, looked up at the ceiling, and said, "Charla had even used the 'C-word' on her in private. Darren spoke. 'What does that make *you,* Charla?'

"That enraged Charla. The name-calling from Charla began. The terrorist split-personality reared its evil head. She transferred into pure hatred. Darren couldn't communicate with her. It was obvious she had not come there to settle the divorce. She came to threaten submission."

Freeman brought out a rubber band and began pulling it, expressing this was inside Darren's psyche. He now had lost emotional control.

I said under my breath, "No, jackass, she came to drop Erika off for the custody exchange and to find out what you insisted on discussing. She had called Lisa the night before saying she was afraid to talk to you."

Charla had stated on camera with Judge Weller that Darren terrified her. The only reason she got out of the car was because Dan Osborn stood outside. Unfortunately, he left with Erika or she might have lived.

Freeman moved closer to one juror, as he expressed how Darren told Charla calmly they weren't making progress, so they should talk another time.

"At this point, Darren turned his back and walked toward the door to his condo. Unbeknownst to Darren, Charla follows and bashes him on the right side of his face from behind. She knocks him over onto his left knee. He never saw it coming. She was calling him 'a fucking piece of shit.'"

Charla was incapable of such an action. She weighed less than 120 pounds against Darren's hulking mass. Besides, the judge had already awarded her a settlement! Dirty Darren couldn't even organize an intelligent lie.

"She was going to punch him on the left side of his face, but Darren gets up and pushes her back. With that, she stumbles towards the back of the garage. She steps on the gun that fell out of Darren's pocket when she knocked him to his knees. She picks up the gun. 'Charla, give me the gun,' Darren says. 'It's loaded.' Charla looks at the gun, pulls the hammer back, smiles, and fires."

Then, in a moment of high drama, just like *that,* the rubber band breaks.

Freeman leaned on one leg as he faced the jury, holding the pathetic rubber band. He then blathered that Darren thought Charla had shot him.

"Charla starts to cock the hammer again. Darren lunges at her. All he gets is a handful of hair. Darren knew he was going to die. Charla rolled to her left."

I assumed all the lefts and rights the defense used were attempting to be graphic and make the story believable. "They both fell to the ground. Charla still has the gun. She is still trying to cock it."

Freeman looked directly at the jurors. "Charla says, 'I'm going to *kill* you.'"

"This is when Darren's terror takes over, and with the dog barking fiercely, he is so afraid, he takes his knife out of his side belt, but Charla keeps kicking him, and he's not able to quite grab it. Then she places the half-cocked gun in Darren's face, and suddenly, Darren is able to extract the knife and plunges it into Charla's neck, once. The dogs are barking, one in Charla's car and Dan Osborn's, and Darren is dazed and confused. Darren somehow manages to make it through his door past Dan Osborn and his dog.

"He's out of his mind," Freeman said in a whiny tone. "He is just dealing with things as they come to him. He sees a cup. He puts it in the dishwasher. He's thirsty. He gets a drink. He sees inventory, some guns on a piece of paper on the right-hand side. He says to himself, 'I've got to get organized.' He is an organized person. He makes lists. 'I've got to think this through. I need some time. What's happening here?' Defending himself from yet another attack from Charla."

It's common practice for criminal lawyers to make up stories. I still marveled at how astounding it was for Freeman to declare Darren only stabbed Charla once. Just by adjusting his language, he didn't have to mention how many other stab wounds Darren had afflicted on her.

Unfortunately for the defense, though, the person coming to present the autopsy report would provide the opposite reality.

His diatribe continued for another twenty minutes, explaining how Darren got ready for a hunting trip after Charla died, which made even less sense than the rest of his explanation. So that's what people do after they slaughter the mother of their child—they prepare for a hunting trip?

I bit my finger hard enough to feel pain, knowing that was my only hope of not yelling out something foul. I could barely tolerate his garbage.

Freeman explained away the obvious evidence of the "To Do" list that Darren left on his desk.

"Darren went to get the gun out of Charla's hand since it was from his family's set. Then he also obtained the knife and wrapped it with a towel and placed it on the front seat of his rental car."

Of course, this explanation directly opposed Dan Osborn's testimony of how Darren bolted through the door with the bloody towel wrapped around his arm.

Illogical to rational thinkers, Darren drove Charla's car into his garage with Sparkles inside and shut his garage door. Next, he then met Dan with Erika for his second trip to Starbucks that day.

What I still found remarkable—what if the police had not come to his place for days? Sparkles would have died from dehydration. His disregard for his pet, his children's emotional health, and the rest of us was the most astounding perplexity I'd ever thought through.

I remembered once when I had briefly lived with Darren and Charla and I had to go back to LA for two weeks. Darren insisted he would take care of my cat. When I got back, someone had ripped her bag of dry food open with spread kibble in a mess on the floor. Her water dish was completely dry. The poor cat had no water and an ear infection. This was my precious cat who carried flowers in her mouth and dropped them at my feet. I went into a rage about that because I had even called to check on her. Darren said he was "sorry", and his apology seemed genuine because for a second his eyes rolled back in his head as he stood against a wall. I witnessed his regret as he paused. But later in the day, he made jokes about the situation and his other persona took over. That's when I knew something was wrong with his mind. I never trusted him again.

After what he did to Charla and leaving Sparkles in the garage to rot—the only reason was he had to be a psychopath.

Freeman, with a straight face, explained that while Darren was on his way to take back the rental car, he drove by Shawn Meador's law office and got distracted. I assumed this meant that somehow seeing Meador's office triggered deep psychological angst, which made him drive to the parking complex across from the Washoe County Courthouse and shoot his judge. "And with that, I turn you over to my co-counsel, Dave Chesnoff."

I forced myself to focus on the next shit-show, as Chesnoff methodically worked to convince the jury Darren was insane on the day of his actions. He compared mental illness to other diseases like cancer. Chesnoff brought out a copy of the American Psychiatric Association's *Diagnostic and Statistical Manual of Mental Disorders.* Chesnoff said, "This book is the Bible to show what kinds of mental disorders exist in the world."

What surprised me was Chesnoff's admittance of Darren confessing to heavy uses of Ecstasy. But their premise didn't work since the drug is known for bringing forth feelings of love—hence the name, Ecstasy. If Darren were engaged in heavy doses, surely he would never have committed such heinous crimes.

Lisa whispered, "Chesnoff declared Darren was on that drug a lot. So why would they accuse Charla of abusing it? It makes no sense."

I squeezed her arm. "Nothing they have said makes sense. It's some kind of excuse for him being delusional, but he's referencing the wrong drug. He should have had him on meth or cocaine." I wondered, though, if Darren *had* been on steroids to increase his muscle building. Charla and I discussed that a lot, because whenever he entered a bodybuilding contest, he had severe mood swings.

I had rolled my eyes so much in court that morning I was sure that I'd created a new visual exercise for diminishing cataracts.

"Mr. Mack equated his fight in the divorce court to the Revolutionary War. If that's not delusional, I don't know what is."

Chandra tapped me. "He finally said something accurate—you can surely say *that* again."

Film crews stood next to their cameras. Lanny picked at his fingernails. Joan's eyes were slightly open, but her head kept bobbing.

Chesnoff continued. "He compares himself to Ben Franklin."

I didn't understand what he meant, maybe assuming it was Darren trying to save the world? Chesnoff continued. "Darren acted upon his delusions in shooting Judge Weller, and the disease he suffers from causes the delusions to control his actions. After this terrible event with Charla, Darren went upstairs and took a shower. You will see how Darren actually sees the individual drops of water out of the shower magnified, like in *Fantasia.* He's in what he described as a superconscious state where his brain is not even talking to him. There is no sound. Things happen. He hears the panting of the dog and nothing else. He sees the drops coming out of the shower, but he doesn't know he's in the shower."

Chesnoff leaned toward the jury and said that Darren operated on automatic pilot and somehow, from that site of awareness, drove to the parking complex across from Judge Weller's office and shot him. The police found a receipt from three months before the shooting that Darren had ordered an assault rifle online. Chesnoff continued to build his pitiful case, expressing that Darren perceived Reno's family court judge as the most corrupt system in the world.

"Darren thought Charla had slept with Judge Weller." Chesnoff paused and took a breath. "Delusion, I hope. We'll ask Judge Weller when he comes here. I guess the only way it won't be delusional is if he says so."

I kept thinking of my poor daughter—accused of being a sex pervert, a drug addict, an alcoholic, a husband beater, and now she'd slept with their family court judge. God rest her soul.

Chesnoff said after Darren confiscated the heirloom gun from a dead Charla, "He tried to clean it, not because he's trying to clean up the evidence, but because it's his dad's gun. And that's in this delusional state. He can't get it cleaned; he throws it in a dumpster. He heads to the parking garage."

Chesnoff explained Darren arrived at the parking garage and saw Judge Weller in his office and thought, "*My, this must mean that I should do this.*"

The rest of Chesnoff's argument concerned Darren engaged in exercising the Second Amendment to take a tyrant down. His lawyer claimed Darren only meant to wound the judge, not kill him.

Chesnoff picked up the book again, *Diagnostic and Statistical Manual of Mental Diseases,* and begged the jurors to please keep an open mind and listen to the doctors.

Judge Herndon spoke. "It's 12:35, so I'm going to recess for lunch."

Relief. I gathered my purse, notebook and rushed off the wooden bench. Not once did I see the jurors look at me. Lanny tugged Joan's arm so she could come out of her sleep.

As my girlfriends closed the doors of the building and moved onto the lawn, we gently joined hands and walked down the street. I needed these women's strength, and they remained on each side of me. "We just experienced a freakish performance," Ann said. "Part of me wanted to pull a Charles Bronson in there."

I hissed, "I get it. Why are the victims always expected to be the peaceful ones?"

Chanda, who continued to have an wise way of thinking, volunteered, "Because we need to lead by example no matter how horrible *they* are."

I agreed, but thought most likely many of us in the world would debate—when is enough, enough?

Chapter 27
Dateline, Oprah, Dr. Phil and Court

November 2007

Matthew Fields, the producer from Dateline, who had sat near us in court earlier that day, invited me to dinner at the Bellagio Hotel. I brought Chandra and Lisa.

The casino's lobby ceiling provided visions of blue cobalt, aquamarine, teal, indigo—a myriad of pink, and red, and amber. This adornment of beauty shimmered through the lit glass at least forty feet above. I inhaled and released some of my anxiety, which distanced Freeman's ugly comments. I'd never seen such massive color in a glass design. "You guys, isn't this one of the most beautiful works of art you've ever seen?" I stood in awe.

"It truly is," Matthew said. "This is my favorite hotel."

Matthew began. "Soorya, we'd love to do an interview with you on camera."

"Yes, I will, with you guys. 48 Hours asked too, but the person presenting the show wrote a scathing article in Marie

Claire magazine about my daughter. I interpreted her words to suggest that Charla deserved to be killed. I refused to go on camera with her. Plus, I found out she'd grown up in Reno and was friends with Darren's former wife, Debbie, in high school. She obviously had heard slanted stories about Charla. Because for a long time Dabbie and Charla were at odds over custody of Jory and Elise via Darren.

"I understand. It's hard to go through those kinds of experiences because they feel like betrayals."

After dinner, we entered the casino. People gambled at the slot machines. Women in cocktail dresses with their upper breasts bulging out stood behind smoking men, who placed bets. A group of young adults with matching Harvard University sweatshirts clustered at the same table, squealing with delight.

In another room, a young male bartender shook a drink in a steel container above his head as we sat and joined him at the bar. For a while, I talked about details of Darren and Charla's life to Matthew. Then, he and Chandra bowed heads and spoke in private. Everyone ordered cocktails except for me. As they sipped on their yellow slushy concoctions, something in me snapped. *My daughter… I should have some alcohol.* I had never drunk on my spiritual path, other than a highschool party where I got sick and locked myself in the bathroom for the night, throwing up and irritating other students who couldn't use the toilet.

My hand waved to the bartender. "Can I have a margarita?"

Lisa's eyes caught mine. "Wow, in all the years I've known you …"

"I know—right? I'm doin' it."

Since we sat at the bar, I didn't have to wait long. I swallowed every drop. I loved the way the alcohol calmed my nerves. Chandra couldn't finish hers and motioned for me to take the rest. I reached over and downed it. I felt little effect.

Matthew hid a couple of yawns. I told him, "Hey, you look tired. Don't feel you have to hang out with us. Please get some rest."

"Would that be okay? I flew in early this morning and I still have to write up tomorrow's material."

"Absolutely. We'll turn in soon too."

Matthew excused himself. Once he left, I finished his drink as well.

On the way back to our rooms, I said to Lisa, "I enjoyed that. It was fun."

She winked at me as we dropped her off.

Chandra fell asleep before I finished brushing my teeth. I went out so soundly I forgot where I was when I awoke. It felt freeing not to be afraid that I had sinned. Now I was a mother of a murdered child, and I drank alcohol. For the first time in my life, I felt no fear of being punished by the heavenly host. If I fell from grace, how much worse could the consequences be?

The next morning, three homicide detectives took the stand. Detective Dave Jenkins, who had discovered my daughter's body at Darren's condo, spoke last. "It was very dark inside. I saw what appeared to be the form of a very small person laying on the ground in front of a vehicle."

Prosecutor Daskas showed Detective Jenkins a photo and Jenkins confirmed it was her. Chandra burst into tears; Lisa followed.

Daskas had Jenkins describe the blood smears. My thoughts pushed back to the Bellagio Hotel, remembering the colorful blown glass of the night before. As I held focus on the glorious lighting, the descriptions of my daughter's blood stung less.

Jenkins continued, "I felt that the skin was noticeably cold to the touch. I tried to manipulate the ankle a little bit, to see if it moved freely. I was immediately aware that there was what I believed to have been rigor mortis present, which is an artifact of death."

My breathing shrunk to nothing, and I scrambled into my purse to uncap my bottle of peppermint oil. I dabbed some on the palm of my hand and held my nose there. I felt a release in my lung passages. Chandra tapped on my arm to give her some. We used it like smelling salts.

Lalli called Detective Ferguson to the stand. He testified about a black corduroy bag in Darren's bedroom containing research papers on Judge Weller's life. Also printed were MapQuest pages lying on Darren's bed. One included the judge's address, and the other was Shawn Meador's.

"I knew it!" I spoke out loud. "That bastard was going to murder Shawn that day, too!"

Chandra stroked my arm. As I took a deep breath, I realized Shawn had saved his own life by spending the night away from home.

Daskas asked if the numbers on the paper were the judge's work address.

"No. It is his *home* address," said Ferguson.

I've read in books about cold chills running up people's spines. This was the first time I experienced that. It felt like an ice cube made of the hottest peppers.

The last witness was Detective Shanna Wallin-Reed, who had gone to check on Judge Weller after Darren shot him. Two days later, her superior assigned her to double-check Darren's condo. Wallin-Reed discovered the now notorious "To Do" list, laying out Darren's entire scheme of how June twelfth would go.

The judge adjourned at 2:30 pm on Friday, which I thought was too early because Monday was Nevada Day, meaning the courts were closed. We wouldn't begin again until Tuesday. What rotten luck.

Similar to a hodgepodge of chickens when a fox enters a crowded pen, Egan, Chandra, Detectives Jenkins and Chalmers, Scott Freeman, and I were on the same plane flight. I subtly studied Freeman. He behaved almost as if we'd been seminar attendees, pausing before the next session. His easy-breezy demeanor was comfortable–maybe a little too comfortable for me.

Freeman didn't appear as the same man in casual clothes and a relaxed face. At that second, I couldn't hold anything against him. What a predicament.

Egan sat two seats from me. "I forgot to tell you, Soorya, Oprah Winfrey's assistant called and wants you to interview with her. Also, Dr. Phil's office contacted you."

I was bewildered that Egan hadn't informed me sooner. Somehow, I knew he had protected me. "I would love to do those interviews, but my wheezing is worse, and it's harder to get around. I'm not sure I could endure the craziness of an LA flight on top of this."

Egan shrugged. He didn't offer their phone numbers, and I didn't request them either. I would have loved connecting with both Oprah and Dr. Phil under different circumstances.

I used to drive to massage out-calls next to Oprah's property in Santa Barbara. I had fantasies about meeting her. Now here it was on my lap. Instead, I could only think about taking the next breath.

My breathing was now so labored I had to sit on a stool to massage clients at work. I had been to several MDs and the first one thought it was asthma. For days, I breathed out of an inhaler. Nothing changed. I was planning on finding another doctor after the trial. When I thought of being interviewed, and was afraid my voice would freeze up even more on camera. I decided not to pursue Oprah or Dr. Phil.

As soon as the plane landed in Reno, once home and despite my wheezing, I scrambled through closets to find Erika's desired Halloween costume. I also arranged for her to stay at Pattie Haire's house while I went back to the trial. Since Pattie was a friend of Joan's and Lanny's, and she made creative fun with children, they approved and that would give Denise and Rick a break.

The following Tuesday in court, Joan and Lanny sat in a huddle with a man I didn't recognize, who kneeled next to them. Jory had flown in for the rest of the trial. His tiny glasses gave him an intellectual look as he sat talking to someone. I waved at him twice, but couldn't catch his glance. This whole situation was obviously challenging for him, and he probably ignored me on purpose. We used to joke together while I drove him to school and his basketball practice. Our lives seemed so simple then.

Authorities had provided Detective Ron Chalmers with an office in the Clark County attorney's area. He investigated anything new that came up in court. One aspect was that Freeman claimed Charla had broken Darren's finger from being her usual violent self. Special Prosecutor Christopher Lalli had Detective Chalmers testify after that to the actual incident. "So I spent significant time trying to identify where it occurred as nobody knew. I ended up going through the phone book, calling all the different Taekwondo places. Finally, an instructor who knew the story said, "Oh yeah, I was there when it happened. It was a joke, and they were laughing about it. Darren said, 'I should have zigged when I zagged, and then she kicked me and broke my finger.'"

I wondered if Darren didn't want to attend Taekwondo practices because Charla had pushed him to go with her so they could move away from bar-hopping and strip clubs. Breaking his finger solved the situation.

The jurors exchanged the crime scene photos. The police had offered to share them with me, but I didn't need them since I'd been with her in person.

Forensics investigator Lisa Harris detailed what wounds occurred on the judge's body. Aside from the gunshot hole that had miraculously only grazed his chest, the judge also received shrapnel that penetrated his arm, knee, abdomen, and right hand. I wept openly as Christopher Lalli described to the jurors the gruesome photographs of a family court judge, with his eyes closed, bloodied, and wounded.

This was the first time in the history of the United States that a family court judge had been shot in his chambers. Darren had made history.

On cross-examination, Scott Freeman rustled his tone to be intimate, as if he and the jury were at a cocktail party, cheerfully explaining the bloodstains. When I thought about it, Freeman still looked as he had on the plane. I fantasized about giving Freeman a gold-plated award for most relaxed person during a murder trial.

A certified fingerprint expert, Ronald Young, confirmed that the print found on the victim's car keys mixed with her blood belonged to the defendant. That was a moment of pause for me because when detectives picked Darren up from Mexico, they even found Charla's blood on some of his clothing and shoes in his suitcase. Why wouldn't this guy have been more careful? *Because he had been so spoiled and privileged all his life, he assumed he would just spin a story off the top of his head…*

The day's last witness was a forensic handwriting expert, Jimmy Smith, who worked for the Las Vegas Metro Police Department. Robert Daskas asked him if Darren's handwriting was the same as on the list. "I've found no differences in these handwritings and estimated these to be Darren Mack."

Early the next morning, Alecia Biddison took the stand. She intrigued me with how smitten she was with Darren. Psychopaths show their charming sides when they want something. Darren had needed a buddy to chum up with against Judge Weller.

After Lalli asked about her relationship with Darren, she explained how they shared the same feelings concerning the family court system. Lalli asked, "At some point does the relationship develop more into a friendship and then eventually into a dating relationship?"

"Yes."

Lalli asked, "Do you go to dinner together? Do you go on a date together?"

"Yes, we had dinner together. Yes, we had gone on dates."

"I don't mean to pry into salacious details about your personal life. Did you ever have intimate or sexual relations with the defendant?"

"Yes."

Lisa, Chandra, and I placed a thumb down low enough so the judge couldn't see. It grossed us out that Darren had used this woman, another mother, so carelessly.

Lalli brought up Alecia going shooting with Darren the day before Charla's death. Alecia admitted she had no clue what Darren had been planning when he brought her along. She volunteered Darren wasn't the best shot, and that she had done much better. Biddison claimed she had heard Darren on the phone with Charla, and she was screaming at him, but Darren was calm. Judge Herndon threw out her statement because it was hearsay.

Oh, Alecia are you bragging you are a better shot because of low self-esteem, or are you setting up a plot to help Darren—what's your angle? I pitied her.

Lalli continued. "Did you ever indicate any concerns that you might have fears of the defendant?"

"Never."

"I just want to understand your testimony. You never told a detective at the Reno PD that you were afraid the defendant would be seeking refuge at your house, and you wanted it searched?"

"No, I don't believe so. I was afraid for my own safety if I was going to be a suspect."

"And if a detective from the Reno PD testified to that, would he be incorrect?"

"Absolutely."

I was annoyed that Alecia and Joan were chummy now, which meant she would physically be around Joan's house to influence Erika. I leaned over and whispered to Lisa, "I wish she'd never come along at the last minute to make things even messier." I added, "Tomorrow we'll hear from Judge Weller."

Chapter 28
The Vegas Finale

October 30, 2007

The following day, Judge Weller entered through the wooden court doors. He had lost weight. I followed the judge's face as he took the stand and settled in while avoiding even a glance at Darren, who had shadows of a beard and was no longer smiling. I knew Darren well enough to understand by his dispirited facial expressions things weren't going well for him. There are those times in history when you wish you could record every angle of a scene to study it for years after. This was that moment.

As Judge Weller testified, my throat down to my heart wept for all he'd experienced. "I realized I was shot. I thought maybe my cell phone had exploded in my shirt. But then I realized I didn't have a cell phone in my shirt pocket."

I closed my eyes and imagined feeling the blast of a bullet.

Lisa and Chandra sat to my left and to my right was Shelley Cochetti, my former neighbor and dear friend. I reached out and lovingly patted all of their hands as the judge explained how, once he saw the window shattered, he realized what was going on, threw himself onto the floor, and crawled out of the room. Judge Weller addressed the jury. "I was bleeding heavily from my chest and other areas and didn't know if I was going to bleed to death."

A woman juror took some tissue out of her purse. My body shook with reverberating, inward sobs.

"One of the lenses of my glasses was covered in blood."

The papers reported that once a detective arrived at the trauma center, Judge Weller told him he thought "Daryl Mack" had shot him. In shock, he got his first name wrong. I was impressed that Judge Weller *knew*. He knew it had been Darren. It was a stunning moment when Attorney Daskas asked the judge to identify the person in the room, and he pointed at Darren. "That man right there."

Darren's chin was close to his chest as if reading a newspaper over coffee. Although he couldn't fake his haggard face. I vacillated between wanting to run over and hug the judge or side-stepping to slap Darren. I regretted not being invisible, so I could have done both.

Judge Weller said that he had noticed two media sites where someone associated him with Hitler. He knew the producer of one site and asked him who had made that remark. The man revealed it was Darren Mack. Judge Weller said the last time he saw Darren in court, on May 24th, 2006, as he walked out, Darren gave him a "mean and hateful look." When he saw Annie Allison, his assistant, he said, "Mr. Mack just gave me the look of death."

Just as I had known with my gut feelings from day one about Darren being the perpetrator of shooting the judge, he had known as well. Judge Weller *knew* Darren had shot him.

David Chesnoff kept pushing Judge Weller, strategizing to make him lose his temper. In a sarcastic tone, he asked the judge why he didn't remove himself from the Mack divorce case since Darren was aggressively going after him on social media. I was furious because he insinuated that by his lack of action, it was the judge's fault he got shot. Chesnoff smirked, bending his body forward. "You *do* realize if someone is emotionally upset and angry, how they could have become incensed when you threatened to throw that person in jail?"

I wanted to place tape over Chesnoff's mouth.

Judge Weller's voice stormed. "Sir, I'll answer your question. I run a fair, but tough court, and when I took the bench, I didn't have to leave my common sense behind. What Mr. Mack was attempting to do was the most egregious case of violation of a court order that I had ever seen. The transfer of $280,000 and the voting control of a corporation, within a few days of getting his own order, said that wasn't okay, was nonsense. And I called a spade a spade, and I think it was the appropriate thing to do. I don't think I'm required to be nice to people and allow them to do nonsense and pretend it's justifiable."

Chesnoff also asked the judge if he had a "secret deal" with Shawn Meador, Charla's lawyer, to hurt the defendant.

"No, sir," Judge Weller shouted.

Chesnoff asked, "That would be crazy, right?"

"It would be illegal, sir. I don't know if it would be crazy."

After more interrogation, Chesnoff asked the judge, "Have you ever slept with Charla Mack?"

"No, sir," the judge said firmly.

Shelley's foot tapped my leg. My invisible character now morphed, spraying sticky goo from a hose at Chesnoff for asking such an absurd and insulting question.

Once Judge Weller stepped down, Chesnoff demanded a mistrial, claiming that Judge Weller had "impugned" him.

Shelley whispered, "What does that mean?"

I gritted my teeth. "I'm not sure. Let's look it up later."

"I think it's about the judge losing his temper when he belted out he'd never had his reputation attacked the way Chesnoff addressed him and Judge Herndon struck Judge Weller's comment out."

I stuck my finger in the air. "Boy, Darren's lawyer is desperate."

It made me happy when Judge Herndon interrupted. "I'll be honest with you. I've got great sympathy for Judge Weller. The man was shot at. Now he's on the stand with his credibility being questioned, his character being questioned. And I understand that's a very difficult proposition for anybody to be involved in, whether it's a judge or anybody else."

I remembered when I first experienced my daughter's death, I couldn't force a tear. Now I was constantly crying, and no matter how many times I fought to hold back, the tears kept flowing.

As I watched Judge Weller walk through the courtroom aisle, past Darren's family, their faces held up high; I saw no compassion.

Early evening, Chandra flew home to get ready to take her boys out trick or treating. Lisa left to be with her daughters. Shelley and I remained in Vegas, took a cab, and went to a Japanese restaurant where we drank green tea, ate sushi, and sat on pillows on the floor at a low table, with soft Zen music flowing. My shoulders stopped hurting, and all the tears had cleansed me somehow.

On Halloween morning, court proceedings began. It was the fifth day of the trial. The United Airlines pilot testified he had seen Darren at the Melià Cabo Real Beach and Golf Resort. Next, the attorneys on both sides wrapped up their cases. Judge Herndon gave the jurors All Saints' Day off.

On November 2, the state called the first three witnesses: A gunshot residue expert, a firearms expert, and FBI Special Agent Steven J. Kling, who reported that Darren had $36,201 in his suitcase. The last three witnesses were forensic investigators. One, Toni Leal Olsen, had photographed Darren after he arrived in Reno. She stated finding bloodstains on his clothes and, that amongst his personal items, there were three condoms in his suitcase. Shelley and I turned our heads and looked at each other. I said, "Wow, Darren, I'm so glad you were thinking of your STD safety!"

Shelley laughed. "I'm astounded that he focused on sex as a fugitive. I wonder if that's a first?"

I added, "A first to shoot a U.S. judge, and a first to make sure of safe sex."

The last witness was DNA scientist Jeff Riolo, who determined that the red stains on Darren's jeans and shoes were Charla's.

I appreciated Judge Herndon dismissed us before one pm. My shoulders ached again, and I longed for a neck rub. Shelley and I settled for hot showers and naps in our room. "Shelley, this is such an experience for us. We'll never forget this."

"Right? Gosh, we've known each other—what, thirty years now? Remember when we first met and your son came over to swim with my sons and I gave him a hot dog because I forgot he was a vegetarian?" Shelley howled from her belly.

"I know—and I was sooo upset! Boy, we've come a long way since then!"

"Okay," Shelley said, yawning. "Let's not do our usual talk the whole time. I need rest."

Darren insisted on taking the witness stand, even though his attorneys recommended against it. To prepare him, they brought in three experts. One was David Figler, a Las Vegas attorney, to help guide the process of what to say while testifying.

An astounding turn of events occurred: Egan shared with me as Darren's lawyers listened to him in private describe how he murdered Charla, Figler thought his descriptions, on cross-examination, would not fit the model of self-defense because of the detailed graphic description of the stabbing. We both believed this discrepancy caused Figler, Freeman, and Chesnoff to suggest that Darren take the guilty plea.

Christopher Lalli spoke to Darren's lawyers that same evening. He explained he would not make the defense an offer because "It would be too stressful for you and your family and create an inevitable emotional roller coaster," depending on how the defense team reacted to his proposed modifications. Although Lalli said he would consider an offer of a guilty plea in return for a forty-year-to-life range.

While these negotiations were pending, Shelley and I flew to Reno. I struggled to be cheerful around Erika, arranged activities for her, paid bills, cleaned our house, and did piles of laundry. Even though I listened to music on the radio while working, my mind remained stuck on what Darren and his lawyers would decide.

That evening, Chris Lalli called. "Soorya, I'm going back and forth with Darren's lawyers regarding the term that

Darren will serve. Darren has agreed to plead guilty. He's now expressing that he will admit to the attempted murder charge with the use of a deadly weapon concerning Judge Weller."

"When will this happen?"

"Monday in Vegas. Are you on board? Because what this means is that Darren won't receive a life sentence. But he will serve two consecutive terms for the murder and his attempted murder. He'll be in prison for a very long time, into his eighties."

"I'm overwhelmed. But what I like about this is at least it will save the taxpayers not having a lingering jury trial. Maybe Darren realizes a jury could give him a worse conviction."

As soon as we hung up, my son called. "Mom, I'm flying into Vegas tonight for tomorrow's court trial. I got the time off, and I want to see Darren testify."

"Really? I'm thrilled you're coming. Shelley, Ann, and Chandra will be there as well! Thank you, I can't wait to see you."

My adrenaline flushed so fast I had to sit down before I fainted. I loved having my son at my side. I called him back.

"Christopher, I want you to know that as we speak, Christopher Lalli is handing over papers to Chesnoff at a Starbucks in downtown Las Vegas regarding the pleas. They all came to an agreement."

"We're close to the end."

"It's uncanny they are using their final hookup meeting to be at Starbucks since Darren went directly there after all his first calamity."

"Well, if you turn the name around, it's 'bucking stars,'" Christopher snickered. "Darren was like a raging bronco. He bucked all his heavenly stardust away and traded it for a death star."

"He traded more than that. He traded in his universal love," I said with a reverent tone.

"Okay, sweetheart. Call me when you get to the hotel."

On Monday morning, while alone, I approached Christopher Lalli in the halls. "I'm having second thoughts about Darren not going through with the trial. Because for sure, he will get life by a jury. What if he gets out before twenty years?"

Lalli told me to hold on while he texted Detective Ron Chalmers to meet us in the same vacant room as before when Jan and I had decided on a no-death penalty plea.

"Soorya, his lawyers will drag Charla through all kinds of dirty mud, and those accusations will be obscene," Lalli said.

Chalmers added, "Besides, under no circumstances will they release him early because he shot a judge."

That comment surprised me because it wasn't the murder of a woman that kept him in prison. No, it was the attempted murder of a judge that sealed his fate. But I understood. We must have safety for our court system.

After talking for an hour, I saw their point. For sure, I didn't want my daughter's reputation slaughtered along with her. That one horrible Marie Claire article had enraged me; I couldn't imagine more. Still, the thought of Darren potentially breaking free before I died unnerved me.

Christopher Lalli locked eyes with me. "Soorya, right now, Darren is in the courtroom early, talking with his family. He's informing them about his guilty plea."

Once Chalmers, Lalli, and I finished brain-storming, I walked back and sat outside on a bench in the courtroom hall, waiting for my friends and son. I also did not want to disturb the Macks.

Shelley came from around the corner and sat next to me. She whispered, "I heard authorities didn't want the press inside while Darren talked to his family."

"Who told you that?"

As she leaned toward me to reveal her source, Alecia burst out of the courtroom, sobbing. She stumbled past us and into the restroom.

At three minutes to ten, the press stormed through the doors and into the hall, carrying cameras and gear. Martha Bellisle, the reporter from the Reno Gazette News, who had written seemingly supportive reporting about Darren that had pissed off all of us on Charla's team, said hello as she went past us.

"Mom!" Christopher followed behind the press.

"I'm so grateful you're here," I gushed as he gave me a firm hug.

The jury was missing as my tribe entered the courtroom. A surge of both panic and exhilaration seared through me. Civil attorney Gloria Allred sat on our side to the right.

"I read she's Judge Weller's lawyer. She's high profile; this is a big deal," whispered Shelley.

I had to smile. Shelley always charmed me. I felt grateful for her to bring amusement into my new, dramatic life. "Yes," I laughed. "This *is* a big deal."

Alecia entered back into the courtroom and sat next to Joan. She wept openly; her fingers wiped off tears from her face. Lanny was on the other side of her, next to Jory and Elise. I looked away to give them privacy.

Judge Herndon called the court to order. "It is my understanding that this matter has been resolved."

David Chesnoff spoke. "That's correct. Mr. Mack feels it's in his best interest to enter negotiations for several reasons. He did not want to spend a week having his wife disparaged, even though there were issues between them and she had problems. That was a major consideration, as well as, obviously, his acknowledgment of his responsibility."

Christopher shook his head, and in a low, distinct voice, "What bullshit. Darren wanted nothing more than to disparage my sister, and he'll find sleazy ways to keep doing that, if not just telling lie after lie to his children to erode their love and respect for her."

I placed my hand on his knee. Christopher was right. But I had to acknowledge that the attorney spoke well. Darren knew he was a cornered animal, and there was no other choice. The three jail cell clinkers: too much blood, too much DNA, made too much evidence.

On November 5, Darren Mack pleaded guilty on two counts.

"Murder in the first degree?"

"I do," said Darren, strongly.

"Also count two, attempted murder with use of a deadly weapon. My understanding is that you're going to enter an Alford plea, at least in regards to the specific intent to kill. Is that correct?" Judge Herndon adjusted glasses and looked at Darren.

"Correct." His tone was slightly softer.

"All right," Judge Herndon said firmly. "Before I accept your plea, I need to be satisfied that it's freely and voluntarily made. Is it?"

"Yes." Darren's voice remained steady.

"Did anyone make promises to you, other than those contained in the plea agreement, in order to get you to plead guilty this morning?"

"Other promises—no."

Judge Herndon showed Darren his signature on the plea agreement. Darren asked if he could still speak at his sentencing. “Because there are some very important things I would like to share because I have remained quiet through this whole thing.”

Judge Herndon promised Darren he would set two days aside for him to say whatever he wanted to express. The judge also made sure his family could testify on his behalf. Judge Herndon emphasized his questions three times, making sure Darren understood everything. There was a pause as his Honor shuffled his papers. He looked at Darren.

“As to count one, murder in the first degree, it’s my understanding, Mr. Mack, that on June 12, 2006, in Washoe County, State of Nevada, you willfully, feloniously, and without the authority of law, stabbed at and into the body of Charla Mack, causing her death—is that correct?”

“That’s correct.” Darren’s voice was now so low, I barely heard him.

“And that was done with premeditation and deliberation?”

“Correct.”

He also pleaded guilty to count two. After Darren answered a few more questions, he ended his seven-hour rant with praise. “One thing I wanted to tell the Court. I do understand right now, my state of mind, that shooting at the judiciary is not the proper form of political redress. Also, one other thing I would like to tell you. I would also like to let you know that through this process, it has been a privilege to watch due process in action. I really accept your Honor’s integrity in performing a very high-integrity judicial process. Even though I have much at stake, it’s been a pleasure to have somebody who takes their job seriously.”

I laughed and then sneered. Christopher laughed out loud enough for all to hear. Shelley giggled. Dum Dum had become the fire-eating man at the circus.

Judge Herndon set the sentencing in Reno on January 17 and 18.

Chapter 29
Will Darren Be Not Guilty?

January 2008

Lanny Mack held an impromptu press conference that weekend and said he "vowed to reverse his brother's betrayal by the Nevada Justice System."

Darren fired Freeman and Chesnoff. His family helped file a thirty-page declaration against them. Lanny asserted the lawyers blew Darren off after their last payment. Even though Darren had openly thanked both his lawyers in court for their "professionalism," as he had Judge Herndon, now, he complained they had pushed him to plead guilty.

The press approached me outside and I was spontaneous: "Darren still refuses to be accountable for his actions. I have seen no remorse from him for his barbaric actions or regret for the profound suffering he has caused. The greatest lesson the entire Mack family has to learn is accountability. I honestly don't think they will ever humble themselves enough to look within [or] be still for a while to recognize that their actions have led them to the place they are in now. Judge Weller didn't lead them there, nor did Charla."

Tuesday, January 15, the court convened at 1:00 pm. I placed my things on the Reno courthouse X-ray machine. Inside, spectators filled every spare seat behind us, and like before, television crews set up in the back of the room. KOLO TV streamed live. Jubal Rafferty, Charla's former boyfriend, before she met Darren, and who had been a Forum Leader for Landmark Education so he knew Darren, was positioned in the front row. Scott Hobbs, a police officer and her other boyfriend before Jubal, sat behind him. Jory, wearing his same intellectual glasses, paced around the room with his arms behind his back. Christopher, Lisa, Chandra, Ann Mudd, and some of Charla's other friends sat next to me.

The court came to order, and we all rose for Judge Herndon, who was there to determine whether Darren could withdraw his guilty plea. We were instructed by the bailiff to sit down. The judge whispered something to a guard, who then left the room.

A minute later, deputies escorted Darren, in shackles, coming through the side door. He had donned a soft gray jacket and a polka-dot tie over a white shirt. Walking by his family, Darren's eyes widened and smiled. He winked and grinned at Alecia, sitting beside Joan.

Darren was now the Dark Star. In Las Vegas, he had taken the Alford plea. An Alford plea means a criminal defendant does not admit guilt, but concedes there is enough evidence to be found guilty at trial. Part of the stipulation was that Judge Herndon would allow him to impart all of his repressed thoughts and stories since his arrest.

Right away, Lalli mentioned Darren murdering Charla. William Routisis, from South Lake Tahoe, was now Darren's new attorney, objected, saying, "I don't believe there *was* a murder."

Lalli said Darren had already admitted to that. Judge Herndon agreed.

Routsis partnered at Mel Laub's firm. It was all one big irritating family. I seethed as I remembered Mel standing at the podium speaking trash at my daughter's funeral. Routsis's language sounded nervous, and completely inauthentic, as if Darren had brainwashed him.

Routsis called Lanny to the stand who said that his family had paid $1.25 million to get his brother a "package deal" to be acquitted for his defense. Lalli asked at one point if Lanny and his family expected some refund? "It has never been about the money."

I mentally belted out that *everything* had been about the fucking money. As a weary soul howling through a hailstorm, I asked myself how could Lanny make such a statement?

Next, Alecia went on and reiterated Darren's exact attack story in the garage with Charla.

Jory was the last person to talk for the day. When Routsis asked him what his relationship was with Charla, he said, "She was my stepmom. I loved her very much. She was basically a mother figure to me for many years."

Again, that wearied voice inside me wondered why Routsis placed Jory on the stand. He had only positive comments to say about his stepmom.

Wednesday morning David Chesnoff spoke. Right away, he stated Routsis cornered him declaring he had made the wrong decision in pushing Darren toward an insanity plea.

Chesnoff placed his arms over his chest and firmly said that once the blood spatter expert arrived, she would have shown Darren guilty based on the movement of the body. I gathered it meant traumatized, innocent people don't slide the dead around in a garage.

As Chesnoff spoke, Routsis cut him off. "May I finish my answer, sir? The other thing was Darren, in preparing for his testimony, had told us that after he stabbed [Charla] he put his knee on her head, and she was gurgling. When he told us that, in preparing for his testimony, I got physically ill because it was the first time he had told me that."

After David Figler explained where Darren wanted to be housed close to his family in prison and to sort out what Darren had said to him, Judge Herndon stopped for the day.

On Thursday, Freeman took the stand. He said he wanted to clear his reputation. Freeman explained how he had gone to the county jail the same night the authorities admitted Darren. He stated that after he delivered a speech about what he would present in court, Darren got "misty-eyed" and said, "You got it one hundred percent."

For me, Freeman's testimony, like Chesnoff's, was riveting because they now had no limitations on the details of what they could relate since Darren had fired them. Freeman said that he and his partner would never coerce someone into a guilty plea.

Lalli asked about a person forging Darren's signature.

"Do you know this to be a false statement?"

"I do know that to be a false statement. He signed it in court right next to me. That's the way it is."

"So the declaration that the defendant made in this case, that he signed under penalty of perjury, you know to be absolutely incorrect?"

"That is correct," Freeman said firmly.

As Judge Herndon said something to the court reporter, I remembered one day when Darren and I were at the kitchen table. He randomly laughed. "You know how when you're arguing with someone, and it's heated, how you'll lie and say anything just to win the argument?"

Stunned, I said, "No, I do the opposite. I struggle to be as honest as possible, to clean up the conflict." Darren had looked away, said nothing, got up, and left the room.

Routsis asked questions concerning integrity. Freeman addressed each with a grounded, reasonable response, describing step-by-step what occurred and why he recommended Darren take an insanity plea. Freeman repeated what he had said to the jury in October, comparing Darren's mental well-being to a rubber band, which snapped.

Routsis brought up Darren's testimony, claiming he grabbed the gun and afterward, and "threw it in a dumpster."

Routsis asked if he ever found either of those articles along with the towel that Darren wrapped around his arm?

Freeman explained he had gone to the street where Darren said the dumpster was. "At a certain point, I thought my client was being less than candid, or the dumpster had been moved."

Freeman continued. "Throwing the murder weapon, a gun, and bloody clothes away were inconsistent with self-defense. It was consistent with premeditation because you don't throw away guns, knives, and bloody clothes. So I didn't want to go there. My belief was 'I have got his story; I'm going to work with his story.'"

Freeman said Darren offered that there was a match to the gun he threw away. "And I'm like, cool, because I can use it as demonstrative evidence, the sister gun, to assist me with his story. And sure enough, I contact Landon Mack, who provides me with the gun and an empty gun case. I don't ask any questions. It was provided to me by Mr. Mack.

"Boom, I have my gun. I don't have to worry about this dagger. I don't have to worry about bloody clothes infecting my defense, and I have a great way to show it. So, I waited. And I don't provide it to Mr. Lalli, through Detective Chalmers, until I absolutely had to, and that was when we won the change of venue. That's when I had to reveal it to them, and they were all over it, just like I assumed they would be."

Routsis asked Freeman if he believed Darren was telling him the truth. He said that he went with Darren's story because that's what lawyers do.

Finally, what we had been waiting for occurred. Darren took the stand.

Chapter 30
Fabrications

It both disturbed and fascinated me that Darren sustained his wide grin as he related what occurred during that horrible June day. He engaged his audience as a performer would, projecting fluid warmth.

Darren took his time, saturating his story with emotion, explaining how unfair everything had been for him. He spent a solid hour expressing how his famous lawyers had coerced him to take a guilty plea, verbally painting red crosses over their faces that would have challenged a *Twin Peaks* episode. "My lawyers warned me that Special Prosecutor Christopher Lalli and his partner Robert Daskas were vipers and that I would not do well being cross-examined by them. My lawyers pushed me towards confessing, guilty by reason of insanity. It wasn't my choice, and someone forged my signature."

Darren picked up a glass and swallowed a drink of water, then continued. "The State of Nevada is involved in a conspiracy to destroy me, and my lawyers caved in and assisted them!"

The room was so quiet, it was like someone had turned the volume off. I whispered to Christopher, "Darren's is in a spoiled pickle jar and I doubt he'll be able to renege on his guilty plea".

Christopher made his usual sneer. "And to have the state pay for a new trial with a jury for his decrepit ass? No."

Darren sat up straighter, still pursuing his wasted grin. "I caved in and became confused because I'd also had back problems from sleeping on a poor mattress in jail, and I had terrible insomnia, dehydration, and was never given proper nutrition, which had led to my unclear mind.

"It was like a psychological *rape*." Darren's voice grew whiny. "I mean, I have a whole new relationship to compassion for women who are raped. It's not just the sex that's taken from them. It's their will. And that is, like, one of the most horrifying things, to have your will taken from you."

I jumped to my feet to scream at him, but thankfully, Shelley pulled me back down in my seat. Outraged more than I'd been throughout the trial, I yearned to pepper spray his face. I thought of billions of humans throughout history who have endured rape and murder: women, men, and children. My family and I were not alone. We were part of a pulsating suffering field of everyone who has experienced individual tragedies, strung through time, forced to endure. And especially now, my family and Charla's friends were filtering their way back to the sacredness of innocence. How dare he express those words.

Darren described he'd gone to his mother's house early that morning, and taken an antique 22-caliber pistol from its case, leaving his father's other gun in the matching set. Darren said he'd been so terrified of Charla, and he went into the back shorts pocket explanation, again.

As Darren wove his stupid story, his voice shook. In the garage, Charla came from behind and smacked him. She said, "Give me my money, you bastard!"

Then she pulled out the gun from his shorts and shot him. Fortunately, the gun jammed. Darren leaped at her and reached for the weapon before she fired again. Thankfully by providence, somehow he had stored a knife in a brown bag in his garage. He grabbed the knife, clasped onto the handle and stabbed her. "Then something happened ..." Darren's voice trailed off.

Mr. Damage Control hung his head and shifted in his seat, but quickly sat up straight again and found his smile, explaining how Charla's blood got all over him. "As I was trying to get myself together, I looked down, and the gun was laying in her hair when she was lying on the ground."

He gave details sounding like instructions on YouTube to fix something. "I had the hair all stuck to my fingers, and I walked over and went like *that* to get the hair off my thumb."

Darren flicked his fingers with that same grin he began the trial with.

I thought about how Charla was afraid of guns and, when they first married, she appeased him by going twice to target practice. My feet felt numb, which matched my heart. Lisa wept openly, and Chandra sighed and kept twisting some Kleenex in her hand. Christopher leaned forward and whispered, "I wish I could get my hands on him."

I thought of my mother. She had expressed that exact comment as well.

For the next performance, Darren switched topics. "David Chesnoff, pressuring me into the insanity plea, was out of order. I'm not insane, and I told him I did not want to lie for my defense."

What? Every sentence that comes out of your mouth is a lie.

Darren's desire to reverse his plea from the Alford to not guilty was just like when he initially offered a settlement to Charla, and she had accepted. Then he had remorse and thought the deal was too generous, so he backed out. Something about the man … he had trouble deciding.

Darren had spoken for four hours by the time we recessed. Throughout all of it, unless describing feelings like being raped, he sustained a cheerful tone telling his story.

I went alone to the restroom, wishing desperately for balance. Once I reentered the foyer, Joan Mack stood near the door, looking at me.

She asked, "How can I get Erika tonight?"

"You can't. We had an agreement that she is with my family, these two nights, remember? Christopher is in town."

"I never agreed to that, and she's on my time."

My cheeks went hot again. "Joan, aside from your son, you are the worst liar I've ever met. You lie when it's easier to tell the truth." Joan's eyes met mine after months of avoidance as she glared at me.

I'd finally had it and jerked away from her. "You're going to burn in hell for your actions. Oh, that's right. You already are in hell for your actions."

How could I have been so naïve not to get her words in writing? I had just declared war on Joan, and I knew this doomed me, no matter that Erika was staying with us that night. I stood next to the window and checked my phone before returning to the courtroom. Montessori had left a message. An assistant said she wasn't feeling well, and could someone get her? Erika hadn't felt right that morning, but she wanted to finish a project.

I returned to the courtroom and alerted Christopher about Erika. "Mom, I'll take her to Denise's house. She keeps offering to help us."

He immediately stood up and left to manage the emergency. I wished Christopher could be in two places. He missed Christopher Lalli's cross-examination in action as he attacked Darren's allegations about Charla's alleged involvement in the garage.

Lalli continued. "Okay, I want to talk to you a little bit about the gun and some of the things you say in your declarations about a gun. You spoke to your own brother, and you never mentioned a gun to Landon Mack, did you?"

"That I don't recall." Darren's grin disappeared.

Darren lowered his eyes and admitted he'd never said a word to his attorneys about a weapon when they first met with him.

"Okay, wouldn't you agree with me that the gun, or the idea of Charla having a gun on the day you killed her, is probably one of the most significant aspects of your defense?"

"Absolutely." Darren kept blinking his eyes. I'd once read that blinking is a sign of lying.

"And you didn't bother to mention it to your lawyers until after you had meditated on it—is that what you are telling us?"

I heard an unusual crack in Darren's voice. "I can't say I didn't mention it. We did not discuss it in any depth."

Lalli asked in a steady tone, "Okay. So if Scott Freeman were to testify that you never used the word gun in your first conversation with him, would he be lying about that? Yes or no."

"I don't believe he would be. I can't … I can't …"

"There's no question, Mr. Mack."

Mr. Lalli's voice dripped ice water, throwing me a chill. Darren had caught himself in a locked maize. He had not mentioned a gun after spending hours with his lawyers. I knew why. All of us on the victim's side knew why. Because Dum Dum thought of it later.

Lalli cornered Darren, explaining the way he murdered Charla. He brought up that Darren had put his knee on Charla's head until blood came out of her throat.

"I never said that second part." Darren's voice grew sharper. He wasn't grinning now.

It was like his horns sagged as he tensed his long jaw. I reacted by clenching my teeth. I knew exactly why he placed his knee on Charla's head. It was to make her blood drain quicker so he could get out of the garage onto better things.

He had long ago explained to me over an indigestible lunch that was how he killed deer.

Mr. Lalli lowered his voice and leaned in. "What exactly did you tell them about placing your knee on Mrs. Mack's head? Don't describe the whole scenario, just about that."

"I put my knee on her head when the dog was attacking me," Darren said, high pitched in tone. I had known Darren long enough to know this was his voice when he wanted sympathy.

After a few more questions from Lalli, Darren admitted being partially responsible for Charla's demise, and entirely for Judge Weller's shooting.

"Isn't it true," Lalli walked closer to Darren, "that if you had seen Shawn Meador that day, you would have killed him too, or at least attempted to? Isn't that true?"

"I don't know what I would have done that day. That day was … I was … my reality was pretty shattered that day."

Lalli interjected, "You told Scott Freeman that had you seen Shawn Meador, you would have killed him, too."

(Oops, a clumsy moment for Darren.)

"I said that went through my mind. I had a thought. I was angry. But I wouldn't do that. That's what I said."

It surprised me Darren admitted anything about Charla's lawyer, but how could he think anyone would believe he wouldn't do that? He already busted himself by having a blueprint of Shawn's house on his computer.

Darren accused his lawyers of telling him to lie about where he got the thirty-six thousand dollars he carried through Mexico. "Scott Freeman told me the best way to handle that would be to say I withheld it from bankruptcy. I told him I wouldn't do that because that would be bankruptcy fraud, and I'm not going to lie about these things."

Darren explained that Ben, a Middle Eastern man whose last name he didn't know, gave him the money when he escaped to Los Angeles. Lalli asked Darren why a stranger would just give him that money?

Lalli smirked; I thought he hid laughter. "Does Ben, whose last name you don't know, just give you thirty-six thousand dollars?"

"He did. That's why they wanted me to lie about it."

Just then, my son Chris entered through the courtroom doors and slid next to me. He was back in a mere forty-five minutes.

I whispered, "Is she okay?"

"Yes, she's fine. I think she's upset about the sentencing."

At 6:40 pm, Herndon ordered the court to resume our session the next morning before he made his ruling concerning Darren Mack.

It was frustrating because I thought we'd tie the procedure up that day.

That night, with Erika in our home, Lisa, Chandra, and I went to dinner to connect. Uncle Christopher and Erika spent quality time together.

Around nine pm, while we gabbed, my cell rang.

"Mom, the police are here. You need to get home."

"Oh my God, I'll jump in my car right now."

Leaving my friends with their mouths opened, I drove as fast as I could.

I called the police supervisor from my car and asked him what was going on?

He said, "My hands are tied, but I agree it's too late for a child to be going out to that jail on a school night."

I turned the doorknob and pushed. Two officers stood in my living room, facing me. "Good evening. My name is Sergeant Johnston, and this is Sergeant Teff. We are here because Joan Mack says this is her custody time with Erika and that you have violated that agreement. Is Erika here? Our boss ordered us to take her to the Washoe County Jail, where Mrs. Mack is to see Erika's father, at Mrs. Mack's request."

The second officer said, "Hello, ma'am. Is this technically Joan Mack's weekend?"

"Well, technically, it was, yes, but we traded days."

"If tonight is technically her time, then I must obey my orders to bring her to the other party."

I shrugged my shoulders. "But Erika is already sleeping. Do you want me to disturb her? She has school tomorrow. It's a long drive to the Sparks Jailhouse, at least twenty minutes back and forth, and we are already going towards ten pm."

I was aghast that this was happening, and it was my fault. Erika, now a piece of meat, had to obey. "Ms. Townley, we realize the time, but we have to remove her."

The walk towards Erika's bedroom was agonizing. Sergeant Johnston followed and stood next to Erika's head. I reached out and touched her arm. "Erika, wake up. Honey, the police are here. Joan wants to take you to see your dad tonight."

Erika's eyes slowly opened. As she became more oriented, she snapped, "Why do I have to get up? I don't want to go!"

Chapter 31
Chaos

Erika, now fully awake, sat up, while holding the bed covers around her chest. I'd never seen her face and eyes so contorted.

My forlorn heart wondered what to say next. As my overloaded mind whirled, the tall officer had moved forward and now stood closer above her. She looked so tiny next to him with his uniform, badge, and gun. Everything was wrong, and the upheaval in Erika's room escalated so quickly. "Honey, I'm sorry. Maybe we could call Grandma Joan and tell her you aren't feeling well."

"Okay," Erika moaned. I could tell by her squinty eyes that she was more than disturbed from erupted sleep. She was angry.

I stood up from her bed as fast as I could manage. "Officer, I don't mean to be rude, but could you leave my granddaughter's bedroom until we get straightened out?"

"Sure, Ma'am, I understand."

The officer followed me out of Erika's room. I heard the door behind us. I mentally applauded her for having the courage to take her power.

My son walked behind me as I went to the kitchen. He sighed as he patted me on the back. "I'm sorry, mom."

"I know. Things are a mess right now."

I collected my cell off the counter and dialed as fast as I could.

"Joan, this is Soorya. I'm shocked you called the police. Do you realize how frightening this is for Erika? She was deep in sleep, and the police are insisting they drive her to the jailhouse."

"Yes, that's the plan. This evening might be Darren's last time in our area because he's transferring to Ely prison. He wants to see his daughter."

Joan sounded like a different person. Her voice was stiffer and colder than I'd heard it. "Let me talk to Erika," she insisted.

"I'll go get her and call you back," I said.

Erika's put on her robe and slippers.

The one officer who had been in Erika's room stood by the front door. The other one entered the dining area and looked out my backyard windows. I sat at the table with my elbows bracing my head, watching him. He stared through the glass to the night yard. After a minute, he approached me, still not meeting my glance. "I understand how a father wants to see his daughter. All fathers need to be with their children."

This officer stunned me. *Maybe this officer had gone through a divorce. Maybe he'd placed himself in the position of not seeing his child again …* Empathy kicked in. "Well, if he wanted to spend more precious time with his daughter, he shouldn't have butchered her mother."

My throat was too dry to swallow. The officer turned to look off into another window facing my backyard. I couldn't stand what he said about Darren. My emotions were too raw to help him sort out his parental love confusion.

Erika stomped through the hallway with fists clenched. Christopher walked over and placed his arm around her. None of us said anything as we sat on the couch, Erika stayed between us, while I re-dialed Joan's number. She picked up on the first ring. I handed Erika the phone. I couldn't hear what Joan said, but she spoke for a minute.

Erika grimaced her lips. "Grandma, I was asleep, and I'm sick."

Erika placed Joan on speakerphone.

"Oh, you are sick? I didn't know," Joan cooed in her hyper-syrupy tone. "Let me talk to your grandmother."

Erika handed me the phone.

"I didn't realize she wasn't feeling well. I'll let this go then because I wouldn't want her getting sicker." Joan's tone was smoother.

I thought about how masterfully she provided a variety of velvet voices that could make the weakest customer surrender to a sale.

I also surmised Joan knew she had upset Erika; it was obvious Erika wasn't her usual friendly self. It took a lot for her granddaughter to get irritated, and I was confident Joan understood this. Erika could erupt cross with me quickly, but I'd never known her to be irritable with Joan.

"Soorya, put the officer on the phone."

Sergeant Teff, who had woken up Erika, took the phone. Joan said something to him, not on the speaker. Once finished, the officer announced, "Mrs. Mack, so are we on the same page that we will not escort Erika to the county jail tonight—and that instead, she will remain with her grandmother, Soorya Townley?"

"Okay, then we will shut this down and report back to the station. Have a good night."

When Sergeant Teff got off the phone, he looked at me. "Ma'am, I do apologize for all the inconvenience. Mrs. Mack gave us information that you had violated the custody agreement, and our commander ordered us to enforce the issued court ruling."

"I understand, Sergeant. It was just shocking for us, especially Erika, for you to come so late at night. No person wants to get startled by a police officer standing above them." By now, it was 10:30 pm.

The officer's eyes watered.

I mourned, not insisting that the officer stood in the hall while I woke Erika. But he and the other officer's presence disturbed my nervous system, and I couldn't think fast enough.

Chris said, "Officer, nothing concerning custody arrangements has been finalized yet. So it is Mrs. Mack's word against my mother's. I wished you would have called first because we could have gotten my mother's lawyer involved."

"Yes, that might have worked better," the officer said, shrugging his shoulders.

I knew he was under orders. We all had regrets about how the evening had played out. "Well, at least no one got arrested, and all's well that ends well," I said, looking up and half smiling.

Both officers offered their hands to shake and took turns, saying, "Sorry to have disturbed you."

My stress released, and I took a breath of relief until I looked out the door. A new shock awaited as I clasped my fingers around the door molding to steady myself … four police cars parked in front of the house. Oh my God … at least five other police officers stood by!

Chapter 32
The Un-muzzling of a Murderer

The next morning, being Thursday, Erika woke up in a better mood. Christopher rose early and made blueberry pancakes. The kittens tumbled onto each other, biting playfully, and even jumped near Erika's head and tangled in her hair on the couch rim while she sat. She burst into laughter. I looked outside. No police, thank goodness, and the sky was its regular gorgeous blue. Inside myself, I wasn't regular. I still seethed over Joan's actions the night before. I regretted that Erika had one more unpleasant memory to store for the rest of her life. To make it worse, a milestone event was about to arrive.

Judge Herndon would decide Darren's fate today.

Christopher saved me a seat near Jubal Rafferty. Lisa sat next to him, as they were friends. Jubal had been a forum leader for Landmark and also knew Darren. Jory was on the defense side. Elise, dressed in skintight black clothing as if she was going clubbing, remained near a wall. Being a sweet, sensitive soul, I'm sure it disturbed her wondering where to sit. All the media was in the back of the room, as always. The tension became like a gigantic arcade game, pulsating throughout the room.

Routsis prattled to himself, pacing back and forth. He exclaimed loudly, "I believe that the truth has been slain. I want to go over how the truth has been slain throughout the course of this case, from the first meetings with David Chesnoff, to the whole agreement."

Oh boy, here we go. Poor Darren, always wounded ...

I wondered if Routsis would bring up his January 5 filing, of the thirty-three-page statement Darren had put together claiming why he had been "brainwashed" and "psychologically raped" by his former lawyers, needing now to withdraw his plea. It was confusing, though, considering if Darren had taken their suggestion and gone for the insanity plea, possibly a jury might have recommended him to a mental health institution with more freedom to move outside in the fresh air. But always driven by ego, Darren demanded to be seen as sane. I knew he was steering toward a miracle occurring and getting off on a sympathy plea.

Darren had asked Pattie Haire to go to the law library and look up how OJ Simpson had succeeded. OJ, a former famous football star, murdered his wife Nicole on the same day as Charla — June 12th, (1994). OJ had been one of Darren's heroes. *He could pull it off too—right?* Did he strategically plan Charla's murder on the same day as OJ did on purpose? Only the gods know.

What I knew for sure was that this husband, father, and brother overwhelmed his family by taking the Alford plea.

Routsis's frenetic spew of words and mannerisms in front of Judge Herndon unsettled me. He was way too nervous. "You realize this is Routsis's first murder trial—right?" Shelley whispered, nudging me.

Annie Alison, Judge Weller's assistant, took the stand. Annie related how the shooting had changed her life forever.

"I keep my office blinds closed, and my windows at home closed day and night."

I felt sorry for her. Annie said she was paranoid, even at church.

Next, Judge Weller spoke. He read his wife Rose's letter. Judge Weller's voice sounded tearful as he repeated her beautiful words: "We still fear for our safety due to continuing threats of violence. But it is time to move on and begin the arduous journey of healing the emotional, physical, and psychological scarring we have endured."

Judge Weller presented details about Darren and Charla's divorce case. He related how Charla stood up in court and spoke of being afraid of Darren.

All of us on Team Charla sobbed openly when Christopher Lalli replayed Charla's emotional plea on the video as she stood. Charla burst out crying while speaking.

"And I have a commitment that he knows where [Erika] lives when the divorce is over. But he gets so angry and so worked up that I just don't feel comfortable right now with him knowing personally where I live."

Darren never glanced at the film.

Judge Weller admitted he insisted Charla reveal her address as it was the law. The judge's voice turned gravelly. He said he'd done everything he could to be fair to both parties.

"Darren Mack wouldn't accept that. And, instead, he murdered his wife, the mother of his child, and shot me. He has demonstrated that he is too dangerous to live in a free society. Judge, I trust you choose the right thing to do."

I could hardly stand myself, as I had wept to the point my heart felt drained. It relieved me that recess finally came. I went outside, alone, and basked in the sunlight for ten minutes. There was a cool breeze, and it helped me to calm down a little.

Back inside, my son Christopher took the stand. "I thank the court for the opportunity to offer a statement as a victim of the murder of Charla Marie Sampsel. I use her birth name because she should no longer be associated with the name 'Mack.' I have had to witness the cold, dead corpse of my sister. Once vivacious, then shrunken, hard, cold, and cut up by a brutal butcher. These memories will haunt me until the day I die."

If Christopher had eyes of lasers, he would have singed Darren. "I have been forced repeatedly to face the murderer and his family, who have no remorse or regret and refuse to accept guilt. The crocodile sheds tears, yet he remains, still, a crocodile. Judge Herndon, I ask for you to give the harshest sentence allowed. Assign Darren Mack to a prison in Ely. Let him never again breathe the air of a free man. Let him remain caged until the day he dies. This punishment will never bring my sister back, but it will assure that Darren Mack is never again a threat. May he die in prison."

I was, yet again, proud of my son for how strongly he spoke. We had walked through hell together, and today, he had his say to the world.

Jan, Charla's father, spoke next. "To me, Darren is already dead. He has taken away a part of us in a brutal, senseless fashion. And even more pathetic, he wants everyone to believe that he was threatened by Charla with his own gun. He says he had no other choice but to stab her to death in self-defense. Even though he had murdered my daughter and tried to assassinate a judge, he still refuses to accept responsibility for his actions.

"Decisions aren't going his way? Just fire the lawyers. He did it twice in the divorce case and now again in this trial. Decisions aren't going his way? Defy the court. Move assets; declare bankruptcy. When his transparent action was not accepted, cry foul and claim persecution by the judge. And finally, when decisions aren't going his way, kill the antagonists.

"In the past, he had always had his father's name and his family's money to rely on when things were rough. Not this time. The crimes are so outrageous that he will be forced to accept the consequences on his own. This time, he will be held accountable without regard to money or perceived social status."

Jan also asked the judge to send Darren to prison for as long as the law allowed.

I took the stand. I felt numb and wished I hadn't written such a long testimony ... the curse of a writer. Now, I was too nervous to edit on the spot. Trapped by myself, I spoke about how my trachea was closing and how Darren had sliced my daughter's trachea. I had no health issues all my life, but suddenly, upon her death, I had these issues. I spoke about Charla.

"A sublime intelligence gave us life to be fully expressed as a mother and a daughter. Now an indulgent, cowardly man has interrupted our path of growth. This man who thought he knew a better plan—who played God. Darren has hurt so many people on this earth. I cannot stop thinking about Charla lying face down on that cold, dirty cement floor of a garage with her shoe flung in front of her body, where she desperately fought for her life. Charla, lying in her own river of blood. I keep seeing how her face looked as the medical examiner held her face up to the camera. Charla had a face so beautiful that people would often gasp when they first met her. Now I am left with how beaten, bruised, bloodied, and dead her body looked.

"Darren slit her throat in such a way that Charla suffocated in her blood. And she didn't die immediately. We will never know for sure, but I'm certain knowing her child was only a few feet away was unbearable for her. The greatest agony was in the surrender of having to leave her little girl behind with a madman. Judge Herndon, this is what I think about all the time.

"On top of my grief, and my parent's grief, and the grief of all of Charla's friends, I must first manage the grief and feelings of a little girl whose trauma cannot be underestimated. There are no maps to guide on this one. This is uncharted territory."

I looked over at Judge Herndon and sat up rigidly. "He is a dangerous, manipulative man, and I believe he is a genuine danger to any community. Darren Mack is a person who has zero capacity for personal insight. Therefore, he cannot rehabilitate. He needs to be kept away to protect the rest of us. Thank you."

Chris Lalli walked near me. "Ms. Townley, may I ask you a question?"

"Yes."

"You brought a CD too? To play for his Honor? "

"Yes, Charla was pursuing a music career. And she was working out her angst about Darren. And there was a song she wanted to sing to him, and I thought it would be appropriate to end with."

Lalli walked over to my music player and turned it on. Charla's voice was beautiful, powerful, and the entire courtroom wept. The Mack team didn't, though. I suspected they all knew it was truly Charla's heart coming through. The title of the Country Western song, "Be True To Me."

So you think you got it figured out
What a woman desires most.
The house, the car, the ring, the bank account
Sense of security … you ain't even close.
You're talking 'bout the icing on the cake.
You gotta live up to the love you made.
If you want to know what it really takes
You better be true to me, don't fool with me.
Don't stray from me … don't play with me … turn away when you are tempted to.
Don't lie to me, do right by me, stand beside me when you're feeling weak … think about your woman and think again. Oh, be a man … think about your woman and think again.
Be a man!

After Lalli turned off Charla's song, the noise in the courtroom was loud. A few jumped up from their seats and walked out, wailing. I was a weeping mess while wanting to look, piercingly, into the pupils of Darren's eyes. I was desperate to see if he felt something, anything—a tiny morsel of regret he could emanate. Mr. Damage Control kept his head down and I couldn't tell.

6:40 pm arrived. Judge Herndon recognized it was late and told both sides to be back in court the following day to make their closing statements. Seventeen witnesses had testified.

Our contract forced me to allow Erika to go to Joan's that night. I mentally held my breath and crossed my fingers. I knew she would see Darren, who would surely give her his sob story. That night, Christopher and I shared about Charla. "Christopher, remember when Darren had all the utilities turned off in the heart of winter?"

"Yep. I remember it all. The tragic part is that Charla told Geni and me she was planning on inviting Darren to join her doing seminars on showing people that divorced couples could be friends. Remember how she flew to DC to get certified for that and stayed with you and Geni?"

"She was excited that she and Darren could be examples, role models for others divorcing by being noble to each other for their children's sake. Tragic isn't a strong enough word. Darren destroyed everything."

That night I took the longest hot bath ever. I sat in the tub and cried again.

The next morning at 8:40 am, all seated, and Routsis began again. Prosecutor Christopher Lalli made his statements. Judge Herndon said he would not allow Darren to withdraw his guilty plea and get a new trial. For the first time, Darren stopped smiling and kept clenching his frightening jaw. Now there was something different in his expression. When I once took a trauma seminar with a specialist, he taught that when a larger animal overpowers the weaker one, you can see the surrender in the eyes of the caught animal. Darren was now that prey.

Judge Herndon commented Darren was "a true superstar and conspirator with many liars as part of a corrupt system that is towering him. Mr. Mack, might contemplate violence against elected officials as a means of solving problems. But a civilized society cannot condone shooting people just because one feels wronged about decisions they made in their job. This case, in my mind, obviously cries out for incarceration. And the defendant is going to be incarcerated for a very long time."

A jolt of electricity shot through me, as if someone had turned a blazing light back on. Before this, there were nights of experiencing a kind of dark moving mold I couldn't remove. Now Judge Herndon's words brought release from that.

His Honor gave credit to Darren's family for sticking by him. Then he addressed Charla's murder. "This is a very up close and personal—I think Mr. Routsis referred to a hand-to-hand-combat—manner of inflicting death."

Judge Herndon glanced at Darren and said he had waited to hear during Darren's three-hour statement for an apology. "I let him go in part [to see] if he would ever say what he never did. Despite that, he never said, 'I'm sorry.' Even in the context of maintaining innocence. There was never an 'I am sorry Charla Mack is dead. I am sorry I killed Charla Mack. I'm sorry I had anything to do with her death. I'm sorry I shot the judge. Regardless of what my intent may have been, or my mental state was, I'm sorry for these acts.'

"There was no remorse apart from guilt or innocence. There was nothing, which leads me to the conclusion, Mr. Mack, that you are *not* sorry that Charla is dead, and you don't regret her death at your hands. Saying, 'I wished that day had never happened,' is not the same as expressing remorse for your culpability in someone's death, and for your culpability in shooting someone and the damage you have inflicted upon Judge Weller and his family, in the physical and psychological ways that you did. And that type of attitude and conduct deserves severe punishment."

Judge Herndon sentenced Darren to the maximum possible custodial sentence allowed by law. He also ordered the murder and attempted murder to run consecutively. Darren would not be eligible for parole for thirty-six years, until he turned eighty-three years old. The judge said he would formally sentence him for his crimes on February 7 and 8, and would allow him to make a statement.

I had visualized many scenes of how this would go for my rich, former son-in-law, who had only known material comfort all his life.

Judge Herndon addressed both our families. He said we had a child at an impressionable age, and he hoped we would put our differences aside and "be the bigger person and rise above."

As the judge spoke with a heartfelt expression, I bored good intentions and every feeling of love-awareness I could muster into Joan's closed-eyed body.

"And hopefully, you don't want to raise an angry and special child who doesn't know who in her family to trust. She needs to be raised with hugs and kisses and not talking bad about each of those people. A child without a mother, and now without a father for a great many years, is going to need a whole lot from both sides."

After Judge Herndon left the courtroom, the guards escorted Darren toward the door. What an eerie, grotesque sight of Darren's face and his over-erect carriage; with wrists and ankles shackled, slightly slinking in front of his audience, handcuffed while guards trailed behind. In one last gesture, he threw his neck further upright to look taller and he managed a smile, as if to have the last command. This was the most humiliating exit of his life. His leading communication courses now ended forever. Being the owner of his business, unlikely to enter that store again. Raising three children who had adored him now tarnished beyond repair—at least with his daughters. He had won the heart of a fantastically beautiful woman, my child. Even his brother Lanny had proved his loyalty by selling his home in Lake Tahoe to pay for his defense. Darren had it all.

Yet shame and failure shrouded then trailed what was his life. Darren Roy Mack preferred to dwell where the light eaters and demons smiled as they devoured him.

After Darren rattled in chains out of the room, I walked over to Judge Weller, who stood with a few friends in the back of the courtroom and hugged him. "I'm so sorry for what you and your family went through."

"I'm so sorry for losing your daughter."

I looked into the judge's eyes and saw his compassion, and I felt he did mine as well. It was a tender moment I will never forget. Just then, Judge Weller's attorney, Gloria Allred, approached. "Soorya, what you said and that song you played was incredible—so dramatic. I'm interested in making you and Judge Weller's experience into a Movie of the Week. We should talk. I think Judge Weller's story is as important as your daughter's, so everything would have to be fifty/fifty in credits."

Surprised, I realized she didn't know how callous she sounded. *Woman, you just hurt my feelings ... And to talk about this so crudely and directly after Darren's sentencing. I'm saying no.*

I remained silent and forced my cheeks to smile.

In the courtroom hall, Alecia slumped in a chair near a wall. She held a cell phone to her ear, weeping openly, and talking to someone. I slipped by, avoiding contact.

Jory spoke outside to the press. "It was about the judge's shooting. [Judge Herndon] was willing to put an innocent man in prison rather than risk another judge's shooting."

I felt blank as Jory's mouth admitted his father shot the judge, but somehow, aligning with his father's logic, that didn't equate to guilt.

I also realized why horrible candidates get into office by deluding, beguiling, and capturing an audience. Darren had his devotees–he had captured his son.

My family, minus the dance and delight of our Cha Cha, would move forward. We would continue to love and grow. And we *would* find our joy again.

Epilogue

Darren Mack entered Ely State maximum security prison on February 8, 2008. The authorities placed him in a private cell without inmates. I heard from a detective that they separated him for safety. A rumor went around the prison that an inside gang would finish him off as soon as they got their hands on him. It relieved me that Darren stayed alone. I wanted him to think about how much privilege he had all his life, and hopefully, his ego would die.

At some point, Darren accessed a computer and joined an online group who practiced an extreme branch of Christianity. I know this because his son Jory and I had a long conversation about it, and he shared details. The teachings prohibited the use of electricity from sunset on Friday evenings until Sunday evening. The church also instructs members to dry-fast during this time, not only eliminating food but also drinking water.

Darren wrote me a letter stating he wanted to "share" his newfound religion with me. I never responded.

Darren stepped up his delusions of grandeur and announced to all who would listen that he had transformed into a Spiritual Master.

At the beginning of 2013, Darren alerted his family that a higher authority would indeed release him from prison on March 11. Darren claimed that somehow, Special Prosecutor Christopher Lalli would finagle the system to free him forever. Darren would walk out of the front door of the courthouse with his chain-free, liberated legs, and joyously join Jory outside. He instructed Jory to have faith and not give up.

Jory spent the entire day, standing in the bitter cold weather, on the courthouse steps, waiting for his beloved Spiritual Master father to appear. There was no mention that Ely State Prison was an eight-hour distance from Reno. Darren would definitely have had to perform magic, to manipulate such a feat—even with Christopher Lalli's help.

After Darren's no-show, Jory still professed for several weeks to all who listened that the timing had just been off, but it would still occur. This vision, of course, infuriated many of us. Last year, a podcast interviewer featured Jory, who stated that Charla started the violence and his father was innocent. Jory also embraced Darren's strict religion. Aside from that, mutual friends claim that Jory looks healthy, well-dressed, and is thriving. I no longer reach out to him, but I wish him well.

The last news I heard from my police friend (who prefers not to be named), was that the warden finally granted Darren a cellmate in maximum security.

Corey Schmidt, Darren's first cousin and best friend who lived across from him at the Fleur de Lis complex (and who refused to acknowledge me at Joan Mack's house), committed suicide a few years later. His wife left him and he shot himself in the head with a revolver. His mother, Judy, (and Joan's sister—the woman who glared darts at me at Ann Savage's house), died as well.

Erika and I got slammed by our rental company, who placed a "Notice to Quit" paper on our house door. The owner needed to sell. Next, I found a house, and that owner said we could stay until Erika graduated from high school. He had lied. Six months later, he kicked us out to sell as well. I finally rented a beautiful home directly off the wetlands, but all the moves wore me out. My neighbors, down the street, Sherri and Frank Wynn, helped me move twice. Even their sons, Fox and Roy worked all day. They were a godsend. It was fascinating to me that Ann and Tony Mudd, and Ann's parents, along with Sherri and Frank, are all from Michigan, like me.

My son, Christopher, took a diplomatic assignment in Benin, Africa. He and Geni invited me to move there and live with them and their children and experience a new culture. Needing something new, I jumped at the chance and joined them the same year Erika graduated from high school. I stayed for three years. They stayed for nine. In recognition of his work on two Millennium Challenge Corporation compacts, Chris was designated as an officer in the Order of Merit of Benin, presented with a flag flown over the U.S. Embassy in Cotonou by the U.S. Ambassador to Benin, and ordained a prince of the kingdom of Dahomey.

Christopher is now involved on a new MCC project in Cabo Verde, learning Portuguese, and traveling much more than before since the family will remain permanently in the U.S. until the children are grown.

Genicia works at the State Department's Office of Allowances as an Allowance Specialist, a role she loves. Beyond work, and besides being a mother to their three children, she is also teaching Spanish at the local library and is looking toward soon leading a salsa dancing class for the senior citizens club this spring.

On October 14, 2016, at 2 am, a spark burst out from a controlled burn in the Washoe Valley area. Because of the harsh winds, a fire ravaged its vicious path over the hill onto the Franktown Road vicinity, where Charla and Darren and their children had lived. Over 3,400 acres burned, taking out twenty-three homes and seventeen out-buildings. One resident, Ed Evans, described to the KRNV news channel that it was like, "looking like a lava light exploding in the density of a snowstorm."

Somehow, like a miracle, the cottage where I had stayed on that property while helping Darren back to health after his bout with spinal meningitis and to help watch over Erika remained untouched. When I learned from Africa about the fire on Franktown Road, indescribable feelings erupted as I walked along the ocean shoreline crying in contemplation. It was yet another ripple in the river.

My mother and stepfather left this world three years after Charla. My mom died with a broken heart. But three days after she passed, and as I drove to the post office, I felt a filmy essence surround me as I looked out at the mountains in Reno. Then, a euphoria-like, and never before, sensation engulfed me. Immediately, I knew who it was.

"Mom! I feel you—you are letting me know you landed safely and are in bliss."

As I announced those words, the exalted feeling inside me faded away.

Elise Mack received her degree and now is an elementary school teacher. She is a beautiful person and always works toward the good of others. She recently gave birth to a baby boy.

Erika was in the IB program in high school and had straight "As." The ROTC also awarded her the position of Silver

Brigade. After her junior year, she lived one summer with Christopher and Genicia and served as a Page in the United States Senate, thanks to an opportunity afforded by former Senate Majority Leader Harry Reid. After graduation, Erika received a full scholarship at UC Berkeley. Her degree is in data science. Erika blossomed into a beauty surrounded by friends.

Erika and I are not close. We haven't spoken for a long time. I have faith in the future that, as she grows older, we will straighten out our issues and reunite. I made mistakes when I took over for her mother. Charla would have done a better job than me. I never quite made the approval grade for Erika. Plus, I believe the Macks poisoned the garden one too many times. A mutual friend of Lanny's said he continues to express the idea that "The only reason Soorya came forth to raise Erika was to collect the money."

I did the best that I could, but it wasn't enough to win Erika's heart.

The breathing situation with my trachea held up after a simple surgical procedure of placing a balloon inside the area and pumping it up to stretch the opening back to normal size. This technique succeeded for thirteen years. But suddenly, at midnight on the morning of Thanksgiving of 2019, it closed completely in my bathroom. Taken into surgery at dawn, the MD on duty gave me a tracheostomy. This meant he inserted an airway tube into my neck for fifteen months until I found an airways specialist to save me. I wrote a second book about my story called *Death Didn't Dictate.* I am currently writing my third memoir about my life as a massage therapist, working with famous people and more details about Charla's life when she was younger. Thank you for reading my story.

Acknowledgements

My story ended with Darren and the trial in 2008. However, in 2011, Egan Walker quit being my lawyer and found Kathleen Breckenridge to replace him since the Macks were still filing affidavits against me. On our last day in court, the judge announced that he was tired of seeing us before him, and if we were there again on petty issues, he would make a harsh decision. That stopped Joan (and Darren) from taking me to court. I want to thank Kathleen for being so kind to me behind the scenes. Egan couldn't have found a more generous, elegant lawyer.

Egan Walker became a judge in the General Jurisdiction of the Second Judicial District Court of the State of Nevada. He was appointed to this role by Governor Brian Sandoval on December 20, 2017. It brings tears to my eyes even now to think about how wonderful it is for families to have his life experience guiding them in court. Egan is truly one of the wisest humans I have ever met.

My gratitude to Marilyn Newman, for staying with me until my family arrived. She will forever hold a precious memory in my heart.

Also, a shout out to Janis Arch, Judy Ogedon, and Cathy Treiger, my fellow massage therapists who came to the funeral and the gathering. I had so many names in my book that it was recommended not to tell their story. Thank you to all who attended Charla's funeral, including Elaina Hancin, Charla's half-sister, and her husband, Kelly. I was so in shock I didn't even see them.

Thank you, again Kimberly Doucette as well as the owners and manager of Steamboat Hot Springs, Sean and Rebecca. Thank you to Caroline Moassessi for all your efforts to help me through those dark days by being my Reno friend.

Another thank you, to the Puliz company of Reno, who moved all our possessions twice in one day.

Many thanks to Mary Levy, then principal of Montessori, who gave Erika a better education by gracing her with your generosity. Thank you to her teacher, Jackie, who she loved.

Also, thank you to those who gave me cash, like Chandra Mayer, Kelli Thomas, Lisa Zaharoni, and Bronwyn Ames Long. Also, and sadly, thank you to those who gifted me at the funeral. Even though I lost those cards, I am grateful for your kindness.

I am so grateful to all the detectives who worked on my daughter's case. Thank you, also, to the Reno Police Department for all your hard working efforts.

www.ingramcontent.com/pod-product-compliance
Ingram Content Group UK Ltd.
Pitfield, Milton Keynes, MK11 3LW, UK
UKHW012253290726
14090UKWH00016B/624